Bob,
Enjoy the [...]
of our hea[...]

The American Beach Cookbook

September 26, 2014

UNIVERSITY PRESS OF FLORIDA

Florida A&M University, Tallahassee
Florida Atlantic University, Boca Raton
Florida Gulf Coast University, Ft. Myers
Florida International University, Miami
Florida State University, Tallahassee
New College of Florida, Sarasota
University of Central Florida, Orlando
University of Florida, Gainesville
University of North Florida, Jacksonville
University of South Florida, Tampa
University of West Florida, Pensacola

THE

American Beach Cookbook

Marsha Dean Phelts

University Press of Florida

Gainesville · Tallahassee · Tampa · Boca Raton

Pensacola · Orlando · Miami · Jacksonville · Ft. Myers · Sarasota

Copyright 2008 by Marsha Dean Phelts
Printed in the United States of America on recycled, acid-free paper
All rights reserved

13   12   11   10   09   08   6   5   4   3   2   1

Library of Congress Cataloging-in-Publication Data
Phelts, Marsha Dean.
The American Beach cookbook / Marsha Dean Phelts.
p. cm.
Includes index.
ISBN 978-0-8130-3210-8 (alk. paper)
1. Cookery, American—Southern style. 2. Cookery—Florida—American
Beach. 3. African Americans—Florida—American Beach. I. Title.
TX715.2.S68P5 2008
641.5975—dc22   2007038089

The University Press of Florida is the scholarly publishing agency for the
State University System of Florida, comprising Florida A&M University,
Florida Atlantic University, Florida Gulf Coast University, Florida In-
ternational University, Florida State University, New School of Florida,
University of Central Florida, University of Florida, University of North
Florida, University of South Florida, and University of West Florida.

University Press of Florida
15 Northwest 15th Street
Gainesville, FL 32611-2079
www.upf.com

Maps and illustrations courtesy of Ramona Baker Brown

Dedicated with love to my mama, Eva Rosier Lamar,
and posthumously to my daddy, Charles Rosier Sr.

The American Beach Cookbook is a culinary treasure trove filled with heritage and creative recipes of our hearts' desires.

Contents

Recipes

Foreword

When I think of American Beach, I remember the hot, sunny days spent at this 100-acre enclave, the surf, and the music coming from El Patio, the Honey Dripper, or Evans' Rendezvous, where we would dance to the latest music and dance craze. The sights and sounds of people having fun and enjoying each other while also finding new and lasting friends makes up a significant part of my childhood memories. In Georgia these gatherings are often referred to as a "Big Meeting," while for us, it was something my family simply did every weekend.

It is also true to say that in many cultures across the globe, important events are celebrated with typical food dishes. Weddings, funerals, births, homecomings, and reunions are all laced with the fragrance of food, not necessarily just for eating, but for sharing the event.

The American Beach Cookbook captures the rich traditions borne of American Beach culinary offerings, and the outpouring of love for good food and the love of history. These old and new recipes are steeped in African American culinary history and were brought to the area.

Our histories are a passionate linkage from our yesterdays, laced with the stories of a proud people, strong in heart and tradition—passed down through the ages. These recipes capture the flavor of that history and bathe the palate in soulful and bold tastes, reminding us of how my Grandmother, who everyone knew as "Big Mama," could "turn and burn" in the kitchen. She was a woman who prepared dishes not only with the experience and knowledge of a great chef, but of someone who prepared family meals with love. Love, the key ingredient that transcends all, gave that extra flavor and tastiness to everything she made.

This is more than just a book of recipes, it is a love story told in food, fun, and history.

Corrine Brown
Member of Congress

Preface

My purpose in writing *The American Beach Cookbook* is to capture and to preserve an important part of the culinary practices that have been established on American Beach. These recipes are time tested and have been made traditional fare by our families, friends, and neighbors. These recipes were created and have been handed down with love, carrying with them fond memories of people, places, and great times on American Beach.

The contributors who have shared their coveted recipes want ethnic favorites (e.g., hogshead cheese, He Shorty's pigs' feet, Mrs. Morgan's rice dressing, Big Mama's fruitcake, smothered shrimp, lemon pie, Mrs. Mary's sweet tomato pie, pickled produce, home remedies) to be passed on to generations following.

These old and new recipes are steeped in African American culinary history learned in or brought to American Beach.

Marsha Dean Phelts beside the bottle tree.

Acknowledgments

This cookbook is in thanksgiving for all the cooks from generations past and present, whose recipes and love of cooking have remained in the hearts and on the tables of their offspring. Only God could assure such a feat. I will be forever grateful for the enthusiasm, encouragement, and support that I received from friends, neighbors on American Beach, and all the champion cooks whose recipes you will find inside and come to enjoy. The patience and never-ending understanding of my husband, Michael, is unparalleled as is the pride on Mama's face. Mama, Daddy, Big Mama, and Aunt Liza were the cooks who inspired me. My son Kyle and grandson Kurt have always been in the trenches to help Michael and me in pulling off culinary feats.

I wish to express my gratitude to and confidence in Howard Denson, a founder of Florida Community College of Jacksonville's The Intelligent Eye Reading Service, and Rachel Deirdre Stephenson for proofreading the manuscript before I submitted it to the University Press of Florida. I am especially thankful to the University Press of Florida's director, Meredith Morris-Babb, and editor-in-chief, John W. Byram, for the high standards of publication that guided me in preparing *The American Beach Cookbook*.

When I needed them most Ramona Baker Brown, Deloris Gilyard, and Viola Walker carried the cookbook to completion. Ramona designed and created the maps and illustrations. Deloris helped me with the interpretation, cooking codes, and chemistry of recipes to get them right. Viola worked with me to present continuity and flow from the vignettes to the recipes. Because of their help, I submitted the manuscript on time and with a sense of calmness. Never having had a daughter or a sister, I feel that Ramona and Deloris and Viola are what ideal daughters and sisters are made of. A very special thanks is extended to the Colony, where I spent the entire month of October 2007 focusing all my energies on this project and labor of love. They were exemplary in their support and encouragement, allowing me the environment to be creative. Thanks to the spectacular Team in the past and present that have borne and sustained the Writers' Colony at Dairy Hollow.

The American Beach Cookbook was not written in isolation. To its many contributors I can't thank any of you enough for sharing these recipes of our hearts' desires!

American Beach, Florida

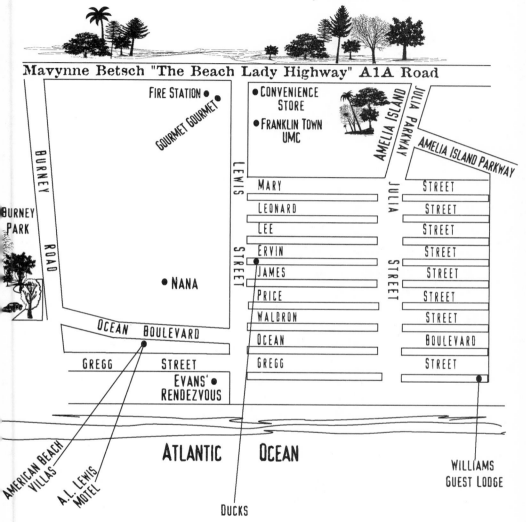

Mavynne Betsch "The Beach Lady Highway" A1A Road

FIRE STATION ● ●
GOURMET GOURMET

● CONVENIENCE
    STORE
● FRANKLIN TOWN
    UMC

AMELIA ISLAND

JULIA PARKWAY

AMELIA ISLAND PARKWAY

BURNEY ROAD

LEWIS   STREET

JULIA   STREET

BURNEY
PARK

MARY   STREET
LEONARD   STREET
LEE   STREET
ERVIN   STREET
JAMES   STREET
PRICE   STREET
WALDRON   STREET
OCEAN   BOULEVARD
GREGG   STREET

● NANA

OCEAN   BOULEVARD

GREGG   STREET
EVANS' ●
RENDEZVOUS

ATLANTIC   OCEAN

AMERICAN BEACH
VILLAS

A.L. LEWIS
MOTEL

DUCKS

WILLIAMS
GUEST LODGE

Franklin Town
Janie Cowart's Remembrance
of Franklin Town 1938

Beach

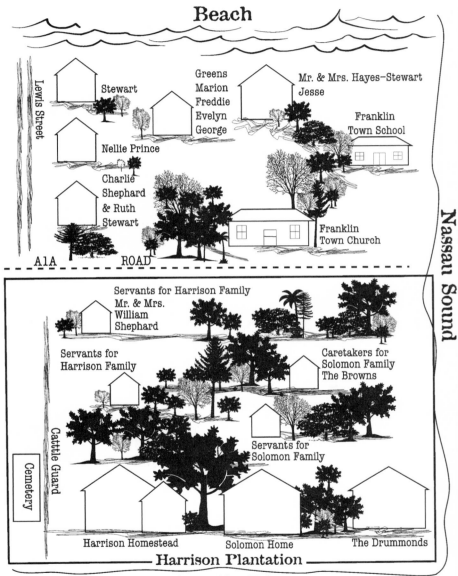

Lewis Street

Stewart

Greens
Marion
Freddie
Evelyn
George

Mr. & Mrs. Hayes–Stewart
Jesse

Franklin
Town School

Nellie Prince

Charlie
Shephard
& Ruth
Stewart

Franklin
Town Church

A1A   ROAD

Nassau Sound

Servants for Harrison Family
Mr. & Mrs.
William
Shephard

Servants for
Harrison Family

Caretakers for
Solomon Family
The Browns

Servants for
Solomon Family

Cattle Guard

Cemetery

Harrison Homestead   Solomon Home   The Drummonds

— Harrison Plantation —

Amelia River

Stewartville/Amelia City

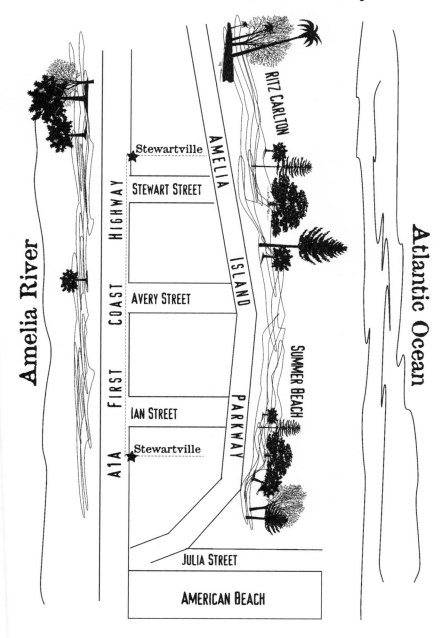

Amelia Island

FORT CLINCH
STATE PARK

HISTORIC
DOWNTOWN
FERNANDINA
BEACH

A1A

RITZ
CARLTON

AMERICAN
BEACH

AMELIA ISLAND
PLANTATION

TO MAYPORT FERRY

Introduction

My culinary beginnings date way back to when I was a toddler stirring globs of food and banging on pots and pans in Mama's kitchen. Mama was a beautician back then and worked her customers' heads in our kitchen. I loved when Mama had to do a head. Those days always provided more than enough time for me to play and explore the wonders under our kitchen sink, which consisted mostly of dragging out the pots and cooking up all sorts of creative concoctions. Of course, these blends were fit only for my grass-haired bottle dolls to consume.

I remember Mama used to say, "Marsha, quit pulling those pots out of the cabinet. You're getting on my nerves." I would look over the floor and inside the cabinets for Mama's nerves. I wanted to find them or at least see them. That was the only way I thought I could avoid getting on them.

Needless to say, for me, the kitchen was the most intriguing room in our house. My favorite time was right after breakfast, when any pot left soaking in the sink was at my mercy, and I used no discretion. This was when I perfected the skill of cooking food pulled from the earth, including the earth itself. I began cooking with dirt long before I learned to wash dishes.

In a short while, I made a total mess of Mama's cooking pots. I can still remember some of our "conversations" about my unauthorized and unorthodox use of her limited cookware. It finally occurred to me that perhaps Santa Claus brought me mine because Mama grew tired of having to salvage hers. You see, in our house, the pot used for the breakfast grits had to be transformed into the rice pot at dinnertime.

By the time I was old enough to tell Santa Claus what I wanted, tea sets, china, pots and pans were my main requests. I can remember yearning to cook long before then, however. Because I had the luxury of my own kitchen set and other needed items, Mama would send me out the back door to play. I could cook my heart out at the water faucet by the back porch. I really cooked up some good eats all by myself then, and my culinary imagination took off.

In elementary school, I belonged to a neighborhood doll club where I practiced my catering skills on the other girls in the club. The members, Marilyn and Jacquelyn Madry, Celia Ann Miller, Joycelyn Nix, and I, hosted tea parties, talent shows, and piano recitals in our living rooms. At these events, the hostess proudly prepared sandwiches and floppy pastries.

My culinary and social interests never waned. I soon learned that my personal touches improved the food, making it more creative and palatable.

During my teen years, I formed a group with three other girls, St. Frances Darby, Roslyn Burrough, and Theodis Pat Brown. We met every fourth Sunday and served dinner at each other's home. We grew quite good at preparing our favorite foods—with our parents' help. Now in semiretirement, we have remained friends and still meet from house to house on the first Monday of the month. We have renamed our group Just Us and added our lifelong friends Mildred Sapp and Corrine Brown, the congresswoman of the 3rd District of Florida, to replace Theotis, who now lives in Cleveland, Ohio.

When I serve as hostess for the group, we meet at my home on American Beach, thirty-five miles north of my hometown of Jacksonville, Florida.

American Beach is an African American community located on Amelia Island, Florida's northernmost barrier island. The small, coveted niche is carved like an open-faced sandwich onto a half-mile bed of sand and surf along the Atlantic Ocean. The name *American Beach* came about in 1935, when the tract of land was purchased and developed by the Afro-American Life Insurance Company and its president, Abraham Lincoln Lewis. Born out of a need to create a resort where African Americans could enjoy and have unrestricted access to the Florida coastline, American Beach became a Mecca described as a "Negro Ocean Playground."

I have been coming to American Beach all my life, as has my husband, Michael Phelts, and his family. Seemingly everybody I was kin to or knew came to this beach. Our family vacationed annually on American Beach during the first two weeks in July at the luxurious A. L. Lewis Oceanfront Motel. And of course we made day trips throughout the summer.

In 1988 our family made the decision to invest in a home of our own on American Beach. That's when my search for the history of American Beach began. These findings resulted in my writing *An American Beach for African Americans*. This award-winning book published by the University Press of Florida has the distinction of being the first and only complete history of American Beach.

American Beach, the Negro Ocean Playground, has developed into a historical landmark treasured by multiple races and cultures.

It is no mystery to me that American Beach and the community's spirit have thrived throughout the most austere times. It is also no mystery to me that the small, beautiful enclave of American Beach, to this day, is still known for its food, libations, and good times. Thanks be to God that American Beach continues to flourish. In 2002 American Beach was listed on the National Register of Historic Places.

The American Beach Cookbook records the culinary heritage of American Beach and is a treasure to be passed on. Some of these recipes have been around for as long as there has been an American Beach, or even longer. American Beach residents and other contributors are delighted to share this cornucopia of signature dishes.

Rather than attending to precise measurements of ingredients, over the years, I have grown to realize that cooking is more an expression of love that flows through the heart and hands of the preparer into the bodies of those who eat the meal. The more I cook, the more I recognize the ambiguity of terms like "cook until *done*," "*some* flour," or a "*pinch*." For universal purposes, measurements need to be precise, but many ordinary recipes become unique because of the loving touch of ingredients aptly applied with creative culinary senses.

Cooking with just the right pan is as important as the ingredients. Until I began collecting recipes from my American Beach friends and neighbors for this cookbook, I naïvely thought that our old iron frying pan was a unique and esoteric part of my family's heritage. But once I gathered recipes, I found cook after cook listing the iron frying pan as a recipe ingredient. Recipes were coming with instructions like, "one pound of ground beef sautéed in iron frying pan," or "coat with flour and deep fry in iron frying pan." For many entrées, an iron frying pan, a sprinkling of seasonings, and a lot of love are credited with a dish's savory outcome.

Seasoned iron frying pans are almost as significant as the heirloom recipes themselves. In my family, a mere day trip to American Beach called for the reliable black iron frying pan. Laying claim to Granny's seasoned iron pot was worth falling out over in other families. Beginning cooks cannot afford to be without an iron frying pan, and experienced cooks wouldn't think of attempting culinary feats without them. The best source for acquiring a seasoned iron frying pan is to ask an experienced cook for one of her or his extras. If that fails, new iron pans continue to be inexpensive, but new ironware must be *seasoned* before it becomes worthy cooking ware.

The American Beach Cookbook is filled with culinary and historical vignettes. From our signature recipes, vintage photographs, and area maps, readers will find themselves on the shores and in the kitchens of American Beach the Beautiful. The recipes in this book are dispensed with love that spans generations. These dishes have earned us a reputation as culinary masters.

1

Breakfast-Brunch

Grits with Shrimp and Swiss Cheese Cream Sauce
Dry–fried Grits
Fried Cheese Grits
Hot Diggety Grits
Auntie Roz's Grits Casserole
Grannie's Tomato Gravy
Fried Green Tomatoes
Elizabeth Point's Egg Victory Inn
French–toasted Egg Bowls
American Beach Crab Quiche
Papa's Breakfast Salmon
Fried Okra
Salmon Cakes
Tuna Croquettes

To eat well in England you should have breakfast three times a day.
W. SOMERSET MAUGHAM

I can remember a time when American Beach residents had to explain grits, a hot breakfast cereal made from finely ground corn, and make apologies to our northern guests for expecting them to welcome a pile of piping-hot grits in the middle of their breakfast plates. Less than two decades ago southerners were good-naturedly ridiculed as culinary bumpkins when they dished out grits as routinely as the morning's first cup of coffee. But not anymore.

Now, grits have not yet reached gourmet status, except perhaps when a dollop of large shrimp, swimming in Swiss cheese cream sauce, sits in the middle of them. But grits are no longer joked about on Amelia Island. In our homes and restaurants, grits continue to be the entrée at breakfast. In time, people who used to be unfamiliar with grits come to look forward to this breakfast cereal right along with their biscuits, eggs, bacon, sausage, ham, or fish. Today, grits are selected from menus on Amelia Island more often than hash-brown potatoes, and to southerners grits are synonymous with breakfast.

In my kitchen on American Beach, when I have the time and want to get fancy, I bring on the fried grits or the fried cheese grits. I learned about fried cheese grits from Marjorie Kinnan Rawlings's cookbook, *Cross Creek Cookery*. Once I tried them, I couldn't have fried fish for breakfast anymore unless it was served with fried cheese grits.

I grew up cooking grits for an hour. Now you simply follow the directions on the package, which basically means add them to boiling water and they're done in under five minutes. The recipes that follow show how I cook grits.

Mamie Shephard was born in 1930 on the Harrison Plantation on the southern end of Amelia Island. At the end of the Civil War, Franklin Town was established. In 1935 American Beach was developed. These two African American communities had once been in the Harrison Tract. Mamie and her sister Minnie were among the last students enrolled in the Franklin Town School when it closed in 1940 due to insufficient enrollment. The next year, when the students transferred to the Peck School in Fernandina Beach, Mamie met the boy she was destined to marry, James Delaney from Old Town on the northern end of Amelia Island. For a gourmet flair, prepare this quick and easy shrimp recipe to spoon over boiled grits.

Left: Ten-year-old Mamie Shephard remembers the development of American Beach just across the road from her home at the Harrison Plantation.

Below: James and Mamie Delaney with their two youngest children, Marion (*left*) and Gary (1953).

Grits with Shrimp and Swiss Cheese Cream Sauce

MAMIE SHEPHARD DELANEY

Shrimp and Swiss Cheese Cream Sauce

1 large onion, minced
4 slices salt pork
1 pound large shrimp, peeled and deveined
Salt and white pepper
2 tablespoons all-purpose flour
1 cup hot milk
¾ cup grated Swiss cheese
2 tablespoons fresh lemon juice

Sauté onion in fat rendered from salt pork until soft. Sauté shrimp seasoned with salt and pepper until shrimp begin to turn pink. Stir in flour, then add hot milk. Continue stirring until mixture thickens. Stir in cheese and simmer for 5 minutes, or until the cheese melts. Add lemon juice. Spoon over hot grits. Serves 4.

Boiled Grits:

2 cups water
1 cup old fashioned grits
½ teaspoons salt
2 cups milk

Put 2 cups of water and 2 cups of milk in a grits pot (a 1½-quart saucepan with a lid) and bring to a boil. Add grits and salt. Stir until smooth, lower heat, and stir continuously to keep grits from sticking. Add a little more water if grits are stiff or cooking too fast. Cook for 20 minutes. Serves 4.

Dry-fried Grits

7 cups water
2 cups old fashioned grits (not quick cooking unless quick cooking are
    the only kind you can get)
Salt
All-purpose flour for dredging
Butter for frying

Bring water to a boil in a heavy saucepan. Slowly add grits and salt to taste. Reduce heat to low and stir constantly for 15 to 20 minutes to keep grits from sticking and to break up lumps. Add more water if grits are too stiff.

When grits are done, pour them into a 9-inch × 12-inch casserole dish and refrigerate overnight.

Use a 2-inch-diameter glass or cookie cutter to cut out disks. Dredge grits circles in flour and fry on both sides in butter until golden. Screamingly delicious! Serves 10.

Fried Cheese Grits

8 cups water
2 cups old fashioned grits (Quick grits may be substituted if old fashioned grits can't be found; I use Aunt Jemima Old Fashioned Grits.)
Salt
½ pound sharp cheddar, cubed
All-purpose flour for dredging
Butter for frying

Bring 8 cups of water to a boil in a grits pot (a 4-quart saucepan with a lid). Add grits and salt to taste and stir until smooth. Lower heat and cook for 15 minutes, stirring continuously to keep grits from sticking. Add a little more water if grits are stiff or cooking too fast.

Cool for 15 minutes, then add the cheese and stir until melted. Pour the grits into a square (8-inch) or rectangular (9-inch × 11-inch) baking dish and refrigerate overnight.

Cut the cold grits into slices 3 or 4 inches long and 1 inch thick. Dredge the slices in flour and shake off excess. Fry on both sides in butter until well browned. Serves 10.

~

Harriett Bazzell Graham's family calls her fried grits "hot diggety grits" because that is just what they say when she announces they're being served for breakfast. This old recipe is as in demand today with her grand- and great-grandchildren as it was with her two daughters and two sons when they were children.

Today Mrs. Graham—a nonagenarian—resides in Los Angeles, but she spent many years as a dual resident of American Beach and Jacksonville.

Harriett Bazzell at a clearing site on the Afro-American Life Insurance Company's Lincoln Golf and Country Club (1939).

Hot Diggety Grits!

HARRIETT BAZZELL GRAHAM

1 egg
Paprika
White pepper
¼ cup milk
Cold grits (enough to make 8 cakes), sliced about ¼ inch thick and 1½
    inches long
¼ cup oil

Whip egg, a dash of paprika, and a dash of pepper with a fork until foamy. Beat in the milk. Dip the sliced grits in the egg and milk mixture. Use a teaspoon to remove slices. Fry both sides on a lightly oiled hot griddle. Serves 4.

Watch it! They stay hot a long time! But it's still nice to eat them on a warmed plate.

Auntie Roz's Grits Casserole

ROSLYN BURROUGH

4 cups water
1 cup uncooked quick grits
¼ cup milk
1 stick butter
2 eggs, beaten
4 ounces sharp cheddar cheese,
    cubed
4 ounces feta cheese, crumbled

As a child, Roslyn Burrough, soprano, received piano lessons from Mary Lewis Betsch at Sugar Hill (2002).

Preheat oven to 425°.

Bring water to a boil. Slowly stir grits into the boiling water. Reduce heat to low and cover the pot. Cook 5 minutes, stirring frequently to keep the grits from sticking. Cool the cooked grits for 5 minutes, then stir in milk, butter, and eggs. Mix well. Add both cheeses and pour mixture into a well-greased casserole dish, 8 × 6 × 2. Bake 45 minutes. Serves 4.

Grannie's Tomato Gravy

JANIS OWENS

2 tablespoons bacon drippings
¼ cup all-purpose flour
Salt and pepper
16-ounce can diced tomatoes undrained
½ cup milk, approximately

Heat bacon drippings in a cast iron frying pan until hot (not smoking) and sprinkle with flour. Stir and cook long enough to brown the flour, not more than a minute. Salt and pepper to taste: the more pepper, the more down home. When it's a rich brown color, carefully add the tomatoes.

Chop and mix, then add enough milk to reach desired consistency. If it's too thick, add more milk. Serves 6–8.

Grannie's recipe was a staple during the Depression, when money was scarce and tomatoes were cheap.

Novelist Janis Owens, who lives in Newberry, Florida, outside of Gainesville, grew up on tomato gravy and cooks it to this day. In West Florida, where she grew up, people eat tomato gravy on biscuits, and in North Alabama they eat it with everything from roast to chicken. Owens's grandmother served this tasty tomato gravy standby daily.

Grannie cooked this in a spider, which is an iron frying pan with three legs. There is also the government pot, which is used for cooking a lot of food, a whole lot of food, enough food to feed a camp. On American Beach we heap tomato gravy over grits and eat it along with fresh-caught pan-fried fish.

Native Floridians cook in iron frying pans and pots that they've had since before Herbert Hoover's time (1929–1933). Iron frying pans are passed down like valuable jewels.

Cooks feel strongly about their pots, using certain ones for specific foods, such as the rice pot. Nothing else is cooked in the rice pot because it is used every day to cook rice for the evening meal. In my family we had to use the grits pot as a rice pot because we didn't have two similar sized pots at that time. A grits pot is used to cook grits and nothing more, because grits are cooked in it every morning, and the size of the grits pot is just the right size to cook the right amount of grits for the family breakfast.

Fried Green Tomatoes

MARSHA DEAN PHELTS

4 large green tomatoes
Salt and pepper
2 cups all-purpose flour
Oil for frying

Slice tomatoes ½-inch thick, season with salt and pepper to taste, and dredge in flour. Fry in hot oil until brown on both sides. Serves 8.

My American Beach neighbor Evelyn Green Jefferson was born in Franklin Town. She served as historian for Franklin Town United Methodist

The Franklin Town United Methodist Church, built in 1949 to replace the original church constructed in 1888, was relocated from Franklin Town to American Beach in 1972 and has been renamed the Gabriel Means Fellowship Hall.

Church, which her grandfather Gabriel Means donated land for and established in 1888. Throughout her life Mrs. Jefferson cooked at the best restaurants on Amelia Island. She invited me to the Elizabeth Point Bed and Breakfast to sample this winning dish.

Elizabeth Point's Egg Victory Inn

Vegetable shortening
1 loaf sourdough French bread, cut into 1-inch cubes
1 pound sausage links of your choice
4 tablespoons all-purpose flour
1 teaspoon dried basil
2 tablespoons dry mustard
½ teaspoon coarsely ground black pepper
10 large eggs
5 cups whole milk
1 cup shredded Vermont white cheddar cheese

Grease the bottom of a 9-inch × 13-inch glass dish with shortening. Place the cubed bread in the bottom of the casserole. Brown the sausage on all sides in a frying pan with a little water. Drain on paper towels. Cut sausage into ½-inch pieces and spread over the bread in the pan. In a bowl stir together flour, basil, dry mustard, and pepper and sprinkle over sausage.

Whisk the eggs until foamy. Add the milk and stir until blended. Pour the egg mixture over the bread and sausage. Sprinkle the cheese evenly over the top and cover with aluminum foil. Refrigerate overnight.

Preheat oven to 350°.

Remove the casserole from the refrigerator. Leave the foil on top and bake for 1 hour. If a knife inserted in the center comes out clean, the eggs are cooked. Serves 8–10.

Janie Cowart was nineteen years old when she began her teaching career in the one-room Franklin Town School in 1937.

Early residents of American Beach and Franklin Town. From left, Louise Sheffield, Francina King, Janie Madry, and Evelyn Jefferson.

Janie Cowart Madry's teaching career spanned forty years, beginning in 1937 at the Franklin Town School, where some of her students were older than she.

French-toasted Egg Bowls

JANIE COWART MADRY

12 large eggs
1 cup milk
Salt and pepper
12 slices white sandwich bread
1 stick butter or margarine, divided
2 tablespoons minced parsley and/or 2 minced green onions
12-count muffin tin

Preheat oven to 350°.

In a large bowl beat eggs with milk and add salt and pepper to taste. Remove 1 cup of the egg mixture and coat one side of each bread slice in it. Use a portion of the butter or margarine to grease the muffin tin and sprinkle each muffin cup with parsley and/or green onions. Place each slice of bread in a muffin cup and bake for 10 minutes.

Scramble the remaining egg mixture using the remaining butter. Fill the French-toasted egg bowls with scrambled eggs and garnish with parsley or minced green onions. Serves 6–12.

American Beach Crab Quiche

ALMA GREENE

½ cup mayonnaise
2 eggs, well beaten
½ cup milk
2 tablespoons all-purpose flour
1 cup crabmeat
1 cup shredded fancy Swiss cheese
⅓ cup minced green onions
Salt and pepper
9-inch unbaked pie shell

Preheat oven to 350°.

Combine mayonnaise, eggs, milk, and flour and mix well. Add crabmeat, cheese, onions, and salt and pepper to taste. Spoon the mixture into the pie shell. Bake until the custard is firm, 30 to 40 minutes. Serves 6–8.

Papa's Breakfast Salmon

CHARLOTTE WOODS BURWELL

8–10 strips bacon (reserve bacon grease)
2 medium onions, minced
2 14.5-ounce cans red salmon, drained
3 eggs, slightly beaten
Salt and pepper
2 cups cooked rice

Cook bacon in a large cast iron skillet until crisp. Drain on paper towels, and crumble. Pour off some grease but leave a little in the skillet. Sauté onions in the bacon grease until soft but not brown. Add the salmon to the onions and break it up to mix. Cook over low heat until hot, 10 to 15 minutes.

Add eggs to salmon mixture, stirring while cooking. Add salt and pepper to taste and return the crumbled bacon to this mixture. Serve with cooked rice. Serves 8.

To top off Papa's breakfast salmon, Charlotte declares that fried okra is a necessity.

Fried Okra

2 cups sliced okra one half inch
Salt and pepper
½ cup all-purpose flour
3–4 tablespoons bacon grease

Salt and pepper the okra to taste. Dredge it in a paper bag with flour and shake off excess flour. Heat the bacon grease in a cast iron skillet. Add okra and cook over medium heat until okra browns. Serves 4.

Charlotte Burwell (*left*) and Gwendolyn Leapheart celebrating Founder's Day on American Beach (1995).

Salmon Cakes

WILLIE MAE HARDY ASHLEY

1 14.5-ounce can red salmon, drained
1 cup mashed potatoes (fresh or instant; potatoes should be stiff)
3 tablespoons mayonnaise
1 egg, beaten
2 teaspoons Worcestershire sauce
1 teaspoon bottled hot pepper sauce
1 tablespoon lemon juice
1 cup Italian bread crumbs
¼ minced onion
¼ cup bell pepper, any color
1 teaspoon freshly ground pepper
Oil for frying, optional

Mix salmon with all of the other ingredients except the oil. Form into 6 cakes. Pan fry in hot cooking oil (375°) or broil until lightly browned on both sides. Serves 6.

Franklin Town natives Evelyn and William Jefferson constructed the last home in that enclave before the Amelia Island Company purchased over 1,000 acres to develop Amelia Island Plantation, a world-renowned ocean resort.

Tuna Croquettes

EVELYN GREEN JEFFERSON

1 6-ounce can tuna, drained and flaked (Both water- and oil-packed tuna work well. Choice is left to the cook.)
1 cup fine dry breadcrumbs, divided
1 small onion, finely chopped
2 tablespoons minced parsley
Salt
1 tablespoon Worcestershire sauce
1 egg, slightly beaten
3 hard-boiled eggs, peeled and minced
½ cup all-purpose flour
2 eggs, beaten
Vegetable oil

Combine tuna, ½ cup breadcrumbs, onion, parsley, salt to taste, Worcestershire sauce, and 1 egg; mix well. Add minced boiled eggs; stir gently. Shape tuna mixture into 4 croquettes; mixture will be loose. Dredge each croquette in flour, then dip into beaten eggs. Coat each with remaining ½ cup breadcrumbs. Fry in 350° oil until brown. Serves 4.

The Jefferson home, built in 1965, was relocated from Franklin Town to American Beach in 1972.

2

Soup and Chowder

Oyster Stew
Martha's Vineyard Clam Chowder
Conch Chowder
Chicken Vegetable Soup
She–Crab Soup
Savory Crab and Shrimp Gumbo Exotica
Red Snapper Chowder
Chilean Sea Bass Chowder
Captain Elmo's Drumfish Chowder
Crock O' Fishmonger
Catch–of–the–Day Fish Stock
Fish Stock
Shrimp Stock
Black Bean Soup
Lentil and Cilantro Soup
Basic Bean Soup Mix
Basic Bean Soup

He was a bold man that first eat an oyster.

JONATHAN SWIFT

During the time when Poppa, Mama's daddy, was working on building the Beach Road (U.S. 90 East) in the 1920s, he hauled wagonloads of oysters home. He dumped the oysters in their Johnson Street side yard; Mama, her three sisters, and two brothers kept the oyster mound watered down, and the oysters thrived there year-round. Poppa's mule and wagon was like a Chevrolet Hummer to him. This was the only type of vehicle he ever owned.

Poppa's family didn't live on the ocean or the river. The oysters never knew this and lived in this sideyard heap until they were cooked or eaten alive. When it comes to eating oysters, our family has been devouring these tender morsels for a very long time.

When we were growing up, Mama and Daddy frequently bought freshly shucked oysters by the gallon or in the shell by the bushel. We would eat the first batch raw with gusto. Then we made oyster stew, put them in turkey dressing, roasted or fried them. During what was then defined as oyster season (months with the letter "r"—September through April), we often began our Sunday dinner with oyster stew.

The Rosier homestead at Fishweir Creek in Jacksonville. Kneeling, Eliza Rosier Holloman (*left*) and Julia Rosier. Standing, Elvira Riley Rosier (*left*) and my daddy and mama, Charles and Eva Rosier (1936).

Oyster Stew

EVA R. LAMAR

3–5 cloves garlic, peeled and minced
4 medium onions, minced
1 stick butter or margarine
3 tablespoons all-purpose flour
1 quart oysters
Salt, white pepper, and bottled hot pepper sauce
½ teaspoon dried thyme
2 bay leaves
3 pints half-and-half or cream

Sauté the garlic and onions in the butter for 10 minutes, until soft. Stir in the flour. Place this mixture and the oysters into a heavy 3-quart stockpot, add the thyme and the other seasonings to taste, but never omit the bay leaves. Add the half-and-half or cream, bring to a simmer, and serve at once. Serves 8–10.

Martha's Vineyard Clam Chowder

SAYRE SHELDON

6–8 quahogs (clams)
¼ pound salt pork, cubed
1 medium onion, diced
2 white potatoes, cubed
Salt and pepper
2 heaping tablespoons all-purpose flour
1 quart milk or cream

Steam the clams until they open (a few minutes). Meanwhile, brown the salt pork in a frying pan, then add the onion. When the clams are done, drain the clam broth into the frying pan, add the potatoes, and simmer 10–15 minutes until the potatoes are cooked.

Mince the clams and add to the broth mixture with a pinch of salt and pepper (optional) and two generous tablespoons of flour. Add cream or milk to taste and serve with chowder crackers or French bread. Serves 8.

Sayre Phillips Shelton and Ridge Morgan of Massachusetts on American Beach (2006).

The sea and the seasons for harvesting conch on American Beach are not predictable, but during the height of our hurricane season, usually September, live conch come to shore. As the hurricane gales prevail, conch, coconuts (from South Florida), driftwood, and sightings of shipwrecks are prevalent.

When I get my hands on live conch in the shell, I submerge the shell in a pot of boiling water and, with a fork, slip the delicious meat right out. Conch, like oysters, is delicious raw. If I can't get my conch tenderized at the fish market or grocery store, then I chop it up fine and make this dish.

Conch Chowder

3 pounds conch meat
Juice of one lemon
4 slices bacon
4 white potatoes, diced
1 onion, minced
1 green bell pepper, minced
1 pound sliced okra
1 pound country (smoked) sausage
1 14-ounce can tomatoes
1 quart chicken broth
1 4-ounce can sliced mushrooms

Dice conch meat into ¼- to ½-inch cubes. Squeeze the lemon juice over the diced conch. Cook the bacon until crisp, remove from the pan with a slotted spoon, drain on paper towels, and crumble. Sauté the potatoes, onion, bell pepper, and okra in the bacon drippings.

Cook the sausage, then cut it into ½-inch slices. Toss all the ingredients into a 3-quart stockpot and bring to a boil. Simmer covered for 20 minutes. Serves 8–10.

Chicken Vegetable Soup

CLARETHEA EDWARDS BROOKS

1 whole chicken, skin removed
Salt and pepper
3 garlic cloves, peeled and minced
½ cup minced parsley
1 egg-sized onion, minced
1 cup minced celery
3 quarts water
8 ounces small shell pasta or other small pasta
10 ounces frozen peas and carrots
1 can cream of chicken or cream of celery soup
Salt and white pepper

Season skinned chicken with salt and pepper to taste and place it with garlic, parsley, onions, and celery in a stockpot. Cover with the water and cook covered 45 minutes, or until chicken is done. Remove the chicken from the broth and debone. Cut the meat into bite-sized pieces. Return the chicken to the broth, add the pasta, and bring to a boil. Add the remaining ingredients and simmer for 15 minutes. Serves 12.

She-Crab Soup

MARSHA DEAN PHELTS

1 tablespoon butter
1 teaspoon all-purpose flour
1 quart half-and-half
1 pound white crabmeat
½ cup crab eggs (orange in color, taken from the belly of the she-crab, optional)

The Ervin Street cottage, "Ruby's Place," shared by Clarethea Edwards Brooks and her siblings (1940s).

The newly constructed Ervin Street "Ruby's Cove" home, which Clarethea Edwards Brooks shares with her grandchildren a block away from the Ervin Street cottage.

Few drops onion juice
⅛ teaspoon ground mace
White pepper
½ teaspoon Worcestershire sauce
½ teaspoon salt
4 tablespoons dry sherry
¼ pint cream, whipped
Paprika for garnish
Parsley, finely minced, for garnish

Melt the butter in the top of a double boiler and blend with the flour until smooth. Add the half-and-half gradually, stirring constantly. Add the crabmeat, crab eggs, and all seasonings except sherry. Cook slowly over hot water for 20 minutes.

To serve, place one tablespoon of warmed sherry in a soup bowl, then add soup and top with whipped cream. Sprinkle with paprika or finely chopped parsley. Serves 6.

~

In a close contest, Daisy Brookins Hunter walked off with top honors and money for her original recipe for gumbo from the Tuesday at Home Makers Creative Menu and Recipes Contest back in 1972.

Savory Crab and Shrimp Gumbo Exotica

DAISY BROOKINS HUNTER

½ pound sliced salt pork or bacon
6 ribs celery, finely chopped
6 medium onions, peeled and finely chopped
1 medium or large green bell pepper, stemmed, seeded, and finely
    chopped
3 cloves garlic, peeled and minced
½ pound crabmeat (preferably back fin), fresh or frozen
1 28-ounce can crushed tomatoes
16-ounce can tomato sauce
1 pound fresh shrimp (medium or large), shelled and deveined
½ pound frozen okra, thinly sliced or whole
¼ teaspoon cornstarch or all-purpose flour, mixed with small amount of
    tomato liquid or water

Daisy Brookins's father, Sanford Augustus Brookins, was a pioneer builder and architect during the first decade after American Beach was established (1936).

Basic Seasonings:
1 tablespoon Lawry's Sea Food Seasoning
1 tablespoon Worcestershire Sauce
1 tablespoon Tabasco Sauce
1 tablespoon Sunkist lemon juice
1 teaspoon McCormick parsley Flakes
2 Bay Leaves

Cook salt pork or bacon until crisp, drain on paper towels, crumble, and set aside. Sauté celery, onions, bell pepper, and garlic in reserved fat over low heat until tender, about 30 minutes, stirring occasionally.

Pick over crabmeat to remove any shell.

In another pot, mash the tomatoes and mix with the tomato sauce, crumbled salt pork or bacon, and all seasonings. See Basic Seasonings above. Add the tomato mixture to the sautéed vegetables, stir, and bring to a boil. Lower the heat and simmer 45 minutes. Add the sliced okra, the crabmeat, and the shrimp and simmer 15 minutes longer. Add the cornstarch or flour mixture last and stir until blended. Serves 8–10.

Red Snapper Chowder

METRO SMITH GRIFFITH

2½ pounds fish, filleted, skin, bones, and heads reserved

Broth:

Fish trimmings, including head and backbone
3 cups water
1 cup dry white wine or dry vermouth
1 onion, sliced
1 carrot, sliced
1 teaspoon dried thyme
1 rib celery, sliced
1 leek, sliced
Salt and pepper
1 clove garlic, peeled and crushed

Put fish trimmings and all the other broth ingredients in a kettle and simmer for 20 minutes. Strain.

Fish:

2 strips fat salt pork, cubed
2 cups diced onions
2 cups diced potatoes
Salt and freshly ground pepper to taste
½ cup cracker crumbs
1 cup heavy cream
2 egg yolks, beaten

An enameled-covered cast iron casserole is good for serving this at the table. Render the fat from the pork in the casserole. o not remove the pork. Alternate layers of fish fillets, onions, potatoes, salt and freshly ground pepper to taste, and cracker crumbs. Make a layer with each ingredient Pour in the strained broth, cover, and simmer very gently for 40 minutes. Gentle cooking prevents the fish from breaking into pieces.

When the soup is done, scald the cream, stir it into the egg yolks, and add to the soup. Reheat without boiling.

To serve, lift a piece of fish onto a wide soup plate and cover with the soup. Serves 8.

Chilean Sea Bass Chowder

MARSHA DEAN PHELTS

1 cup minced onions
1 cup minced green bell pepper
2 hot peppers
2 cups cooked sliced carrots
1 quart water (fish stock preferred; see p. 35)
⅓ cup cornstarch
1 quart milk or cream, divided
Salt and pepper
1½ pounds Chilean sea bass fillets, skinned
4 tablespoons butter or margarine

Place onions, bell pepper, hot peppers, and cooked carrots in a 5-quart stockpot with one quart of water and bring to a full boil. Lower heat and simmer for 45 minutes.

Mix cornstarch in 1 cup of the milk or cream, then stir it into the simmering stock. Increase the heat slightly and add the remaining milk or cream. When the broth is nearly at a boil, add the fish that has been seasoned with salt and pepper and butter or margarine. Reduce heat and simmer for 20 minutes, or until fish flakes easily with a fork. Serves 8–10.

Captain Elmo's Drumfish Chowder

ANNETTE MCCOLLOUGH MYERS

1 large onion, minced
4 ribs celery, sliced
1 large green bell pepper, minced
3 tablespoons vegetable oil or butter
3 17-ounce cans crushed tomatoes
2 quarts fish stock or water (see p. 35)
1 teaspoon dried thyme
2 bay leaves
4 cloves garlic, peeled and minced
4 carrots, sliced
4 potatoes, quartered

Salt and hot peppers
1 10-ounce box frozen English peas, thawed
3 pounds drumfish fillets

Sauté onions, celery, and bell pepper in oil or butter until tender but not brown. Pour the vegetables into a large stockpot. Add tomatoes and fish stock or water followed by thyme, bay leaves, garlic, carrots, potatoes, and salt and hot peppers to taste. Simmer for 20 minutes, then add peas and drumfish fillets. Remove skin from fish if it has not been previously removed by way of cutting fish into fillets. Simmer for 10 minutes. Let rest 10 minutes before serving. Serves 12.

When Captain Elmo was in South America, cubed chunks of pumpkin or turnip roots were added to the chowder.

At home with shrimp boat Captain and Mrs. Elmo (Annette) Myers (1965).

Crock O'Fishmonger

RONALD MILLER

2 quarts fish or shrimp stock (see p. 35)
1 cup minced green bell pepper
1 cup minced onions
1 tablespoon cornstarch
2 quarts half-and-half, divided
1 tablespoon butter
Few drops onion juice
White pepper
½ teaspoon Worcestershire sauce
½ teaspoon sea salt
1 pound crab claw meat
1 pound steamed flounder or any white fish, cut in chunks
½ cup dry sherry

Place fish or shrimp stock in a large pot with the bell peppers and onions. Bring to a boil, lower heat, and simmer approximately 30 minutes.

Blend cornstarch with ½ cup half-and-half until smooth. Add remaining half-and-half, the cornstarch paste, butter, onion juice, ground white pepper, Worcestershire sauce, and sea salt to the stockpot. Simmer 15 minutes.

Season the steamed fish with salt and white pepper to taste. Place fish and crab claws in a 5-quart slow cooker. Pour stock over fish and crabmeat, cover, and cook on low for 15 minutes. When ready to serve, add sherry, stir, and enjoy the slurping sounds from all around. Serves 12.

Catch-of-the-Day Fish Stock

MARSHA DEAN PHELTS

When Fish Man from Mayport pulls up to the door early in the morning or at dusk with irresistible prices, it means buyers are in for a long day of cleaning and prepping the catch for storage or a fish fry right away. In an effort to unload his catch and get home to bed, Fish Man drops the price.

Mentally, I race to find the earliest date or occasion for having a fish fry. The fish comes in a range of sizes and types. I clean and separate fish types into batches for cooking. A lot of scrap meat will come from the heads of the bigger fish. I separate the edible scraps, which include the backbone.

Fish Stock

To make fish stock, remove the gills from the fish heads. Season the fish heads and backbone with salt and pepper to taste and one or two fresh onions minced. Add enough water to cover fish parts by 1 inch, bring water to a boil, lower the heat, and simmer for no more than 20 minutes. Don't overcook. Leave the heads and backbone in the stock until cool.

Remove meat from the heads and backbone and save for making fish-wiches or a crock o'fishmonger. Strain the fish stock into sterilized quart or half-gallon containers. Freeze until needed for crock o'fishmonger and other seafood-based stocks, stews, and soups. Makes 1 gallon or more.

Shrimp Stock

To make shrimp stock, snap the heads from about 5 pounds of shrimp. With fresh shrimp, while squeezing, pull the head from the body with the thumb and index finger; the waste string will come straight from the spine without using a deveining tool.

Wash the heads and place them in a large stockpot with enough water to cover. Season if you must (but these heads have a wonderfully pungent flavor of their own) with salt, pepper, and one or two minced raw onions. Bring to a boil, lower the heat to low, and simmer slowly for 2 hours. When the stock has cooled, strain it and pour it into sterilized quart or half-gallon containers and freeze until ready to make seafood soup, stew, or chowder. You'll be so glad that you did.

Dr. Johnnetta Betsch Cole, the 2004–2006 national chairwoman of the United Way of America, is the great-granddaughter of Abraham Lincoln Lewis, the founding principal and visionary for American Beach.

Without the vision of A. L. Lewis, there would be no American Beach. He was one of seven founders of the Afro-American Life Insurance Company, which established American Beach in 1935, and the first black insurance company in the state of Florida in 1901.

As Lewis's oldest surviving descendant, Johnnetta Betsch Cole has become the family matriarch. She became most noted as president of the prestigious Spelman College in Atlanta and of Bennett College for Women in Greensboro, North Carolina. Dr. Cole is beloved as sister, mother, grandmother, aunt, and friend. She is also acclaimed for her culinary feats.

Black Bean Soup

JOHNNETTA BETSCH COLE

1 pound dried black beans
2 quarts water
⅔ cup olive oil
6 cloves garlic, peeled and minced
2 onions, peeled and finely chopped
¼ teaspoon dried oregano
½ teaspoon ground cumin
¼ teaspoon ground coriander
2 bay leaves
Salt and pepper
Red pepper or bottled hot pepper sauce
2 tablespoons dry red wine
Cooked brown rice, optional

American Beach property owners Florida state senator Tony Hill and Dr. Johnnetta Betsch Cole at the dedication and renaming of a portion of Highway A1A (2006).

Johnnetta Betsch in a fashionable two-piece bathing suit on the hood of her father's car (1949).

Pick over the beans, discarding any shriveled ones or foreign particles. Wash well and soak overnight in water that generously covers the beans.

Drain the beans, rinse in fresh water, and drain again. Place the beans in a cooking pot with 2 quarts of water. Bring to a rapid boil, reduce heat to medium, cover, and cook about 45 minutes.

In a skillet, heat the olive oil until hot but not smoking and sauté the garlic and onions for 10 minutes over low heat. Add 1 cup of the drained black beans and mash thoroughly with the rest of the ingredients in the skillet. Add this mixture to the cooking pot together with the oregano, cumin, coriander, bay leaves, salt and pepper to taste, and red pepper or hot pepper sauce to taste. Cover and cook for 1 hour over medium heat. Add the red wine and cook over low heat for 1 hour. Uncover the pot and cook until the soup thickens to taste. Serve in bowls or soup plates, or serve over brown rice. Serves 4–6.

Lentil and Cilantro Soup

GLORIA AND CHARLIE RODERICK

1 tablespoon oil
½ cup minced red onions
1 garlic clove, minced
2½ cups chicken stock
½ cup brown lentils
1 teaspoon sea salt
1 teaspoon black pepper
½ cup peeled and minced carrots
1 cup cubed ham
2 tablespoons minced fresh cilantro
Plain yogurt or sour cream for garnish, optional
Minced cilantro, for garnish

Heat the oil in a saucepan and sauté the onions until soft. Add garlic and stir for 1 minute. Add stock, lentils, salt, pepper, and carrots and bring to a simmer. Add ham and cook for 30 minutes. Top with a dab of yogurt or sour cream and cilantro, then enjoy. Serves 4.

Basic Bean Soup Mix

MARSHA DEAN PHELTS

1 cup small dried red beans
1 cup dried black beans
½ cup dried kidney beans
½ cup dried chickpeas
½ cup dried pinto beans
½ cup dried yellow-eye peas
½ cup navy beans
½ cup dried baby lima beans
½ cup dried black-eyed peas
½ cup dried yellow split peas
½ cup dried green split peas
½ cup dried green lentils
½ cup dried red lentils

Seasoning Packet:

4 tablespoons dehydrated minced onion
4 teaspoons dried celery flakes
4 bay leaves, broken
4 teaspoons granulated garlic
2 tablespoons dried parsley
2 teaspoons dried oregano
2 teaspoons dried basil
2 teaspoons cumin
1 teaspoon chili powder
1 teaspoon red pepper
1 teaspoon white pepper
2 teaspoons black pepper

Combine dried beans, peas, and lentils in a bowl and mix well. Divide and place in 4 pint jars. Divide the seasoning into 4 packets, seal each in a plastic bag, and place 1 packet in each jar.

Basic Bean Soup

2 cups bean soup mix
2 tablespoons seasoning mix
8 cups water
2 cups beef broth
2 cups chunky tomato sauce (or prepared spaghetti sauce)
½ pound smoked sausage or ham, minced
Salt
1 tablespoon lemon juice
½ cup finely chopped parsley
½ cup finely chopped green onion

Rinse beans, then soak 6 hours or overnight in water to cover. Drain.

Combine beans with water, broth, tomato sauce, seasoning mix and meat in a soup pot and bring to a boil. Reduce heat and simmer for 2 hours, or until beans are tender, adding water if necessary.

Add salt to taste in the last ½ hour of cooking. Before serving, stir in the lemon juice, parsley, and green onion. Serves 8.

3

Party Hearty Appetizers

Durham's Cocktail Wieners

Beer Ball

Chopped Chicken Livers

Deep–fried Chicken Livers

He Shorty's Pigs' Feet

Hogshead Cheese

Boiled Tongue

Spinach Balls

Spinach Dip

Love and Joy Oyster Dip

Avocado Crab Dip

Shrimp Dip

Tipsy Shrimp Spread

Black Man's Ambrosia

Red Deviled Spiced Shrimp
and Sauce

Crab and Shrimp Poppers

Pickled Shrimp

Crab Dabs

Aunt Liza's Sardine Supremes

Cheese Bites

Cheese Straws

Cheese Crisps

Cheese Puffs

Petronella's Crab–stuffed Eggs

Southern–style Deviled Eggs

Tomato Pizza

Peppered Pecans

Glazed Nuts

Appetite comes with eating.

FRENCH PROVERB

The Durhams are a warm, outgoing, and popular family. The many entrepreneurial efforts of Ben, Sr., and his wife, Evelena, afforded the family a lifestyle that many could only wistfully dream about. While the five boys and four girls were growing up in Jacksonville, their parents owned and operated a gas station, restaurant, Laundromat, and rental properties. The Durham clan vacationed and enjoyed recreation on American Beach. From racing cars, motorcycles, and speedboats to water skiing and fishing, they lit up American Beach.

They had huge and fabulous gatherings for family and friends. There was an abundance of choice foods, a contagious spirit of hospitality, and competitive card playing. When Gladys Durham Nelson raised the flag on American Beach, a party was sure to follow. This recipe dates back to 1966. Cocktail wieners were pricier at that time, thus hot dogs were used instead.

Skeeter Miller (*left*) and Mabel Ward having a taste during cocktail hour on American Beach (circa 1950s).

Durham's Cocktail Wieners

1 cup bourbon
1 cup catsup
½ cup firmly packed light brown sugar
1 tablespoon minced onion
2 teaspoons Worcestershire sauce
⅛ teaspoon bottled hot pepper sauce
1 pound hot dogs (or 14 ounce package cocktail wieners)

Combine bourbon, catsup, brown sugar, onion, Worcestershire sauce, and hot pepper sauce in a saucepan. Bring to a boil, lower heat, and simmer, uncovered, 30 minutes, stirring occasionally. Cut hot dogs into quarters (if using cocktail wieners, no need to cut them). Add to sauce and simmer 30 minutes more. Serve hot in a casserole or on a platter. Either choice of cocktail wieners or hot dogs makes 40 pieces.

Beer Ball

MARSHA DEAN PHELTS

1½ pounds liverwurst
½ cup mayonnaise
1 small onion, grated
1 teaspoon prepared horseradish
1 tablespoon dry mustard
4 ounces beer, divided
8 ounces cream cheese, softened
1 tablespoon bottled hot pepper sauce
½ cup minced parsley

In a mixing bowl, mash liverwurst with a fork. Stir in mayonnaise to soften, then add onion, horseradish, dry mustard, 2 ounces beer, and hot pepper sauce. Mix well and shape into one large ball or two smaller ones. Mixture should hold its shape when rolled into a ball. Refrigerate for 30 minutes.

Combine cream cheese with remaining 2 ounces of beer and spread over liverwurst ball(s). Roll ball(s) in minced parsley and refrigerate overnight.

This tasty hors d'oeuvres freezes well. Serve with an assortment of crackers. Serves 8.

Chopped Chicken Livers

CLAIRE KOSHAR

1½ medium onions, sliced, divided
1 pound chicken livers
1 small slice rye bread
4 hard-boiled eggs, peeled
¼ cup chicken fat, melted
Salt, garlic salt, paprika, and pepper to taste

Sauté half an onion. Lightly season chicken livers with salt and pepper and sauté in chicken fat until done, approximately 6–8 minutes but still soft. Put chicken livers, sautéed onions, remaining sliced onions, the rye bread, and hard-boiled eggs through a meat grinder. Mix the ground mixture well with the melted chicken fat and additional seasonings to taste. Refrigerate until cold. Serve over bread or crackers. Serves 8–10.

Deep-fried Chicken Livers

MARSHA DEAN PHELTS

1 pound chicken livers
Salt and pepper
½ cup all-purpose flour
2 cups oil

Season chicken livers with salt and pepper to taste and dredge in flour. Shake off excess flour. Heat oil until hot but not smoking. Drop chicken livers in hot oil. When they float to the top of the pan, remove them and serve immediately. Serves 4.

I know of no polite way to eat this delicacy. Those who serve or enjoy this are not finicky eaters. This is an authentic dish of the South. Without couth, I treat barbecued pigs' feet as a finger food and approach them the same way I do boiled blue crabs or a Hayden mango. That is, I eat them from hand to mouth, from beginning to end. My friend the late Samuel Lee Thompson taught me how to prepare this dish. This recipe can also be found in my first book, *An American Beach for African Americans.*

He Shorty's Pigs' Feet

SAMUEL LEE THOMPSON

12 pigs' feet, split in half lengthwise and well washed
2 cups white vinegar
2 tablespoons salt
1 tablespoon pepper

Barbecue Sauce:

1 quart catsup
1 pint yellow mustard
1 tablespoon salt
¼ cup crushed red pepper flakes
2 tablespoons chili powder
1 tablespoon garlic powder
¼ cup sugar
¼ cup white vinegar

Place cleaned pigs' feet in a heavy 12-quart stockpot. Cover with water and 2 cups of vinegar. Add salt and pepper, bring to a full boil, lower heat to medium, and cook for 2 hours.

Prepare sauce by mixing all ingredients together.

Preheat oven to 300°.

Remove pigs' feet from pot, coat each one in the special barbecue sauce, and arrange in a single layer in a roasting pan. Bake 2 hours uncovered, or until tender, basting frequently. Serves 4–6.

Lougenia "Jeannie" Harris is a master cook. She has an oceanfront garden outside her door. Jeannie's husband, James, a native of Amelia Island, comes by all the seafood, game, and fresh roadkill one could wish for. Because of changing times, recipes for roadkill and backyard critters are not included in this cookbook; however, American Beach people continue to cook from the land. This picture was selected because Lougenia Harris is the Lougenia Caldwell in the photo with American Beach friends in the 1940s.

Preparing hogshead cheese is a wintertime ritual in many beach households. Homemade hogshead cheese is as traditional as the Thanksgiving turkey.

American Beach residents Pasco and Lougenia Caldwell (*left*), Henry Myers, and Dorothy and Tommy Jordan at New York City's Birdland Jazz Club (circa 1940s).

Hogshead Cheese

LOUGENIA JACKSON HARRIS

1 hogshead, quartered by butcher	1 bunch celery, minced
3 tablespoons ground sage	2 green bell peppers, minced
3 tablespoons ground thyme	Salt and pepper
½ cup lemon juice	5–6 hot peppers
5 cloves garlic, peeled and minced	3 pounds pigs' ears
2–3 bay leaves	3 pounds pigs' feet
1 tablespoon ground oregano	2 cups white vinegar
2 large onions	

Remove and discard the eyes from the hogshead. Remove the brain and reserve for another use. Skin the cooked tongue. Place the hogshead tongue included in a stockpot and cover with water. Add sage, thyme, lemon juice, garlic, bay leaves, oregano, onions, celery, bell peppers, salt and pepper to taste, and hot peppers and bring to a boil. Boil until meat pulls away from the bones, approximately 3 hours. Place the pig ears and pigs' feet in another stockpot, cover with water, and bring to a boil. Boil until the meat can be easily removed from bones approximately two hours.

Remove meat from the pots, pull cooked meat from the bones, combine well, and mince. Divide minced meats into two 9-inch × 13-inch casserole dishes. Add 1 cup of vinegar to each casserole dish, cover, and refrigerate overnight.

Slice thinly and place on a bed of lettuce on a serving dish flanked with crackers. Serves 25.

The wedding party of I. H. Burney and Miriam Cunningham (1936). The Burneys honeymooned on American Beach, and he eventually became president of the Afro-American Life Insurance Company.

Isadore H. Burney and his bride, Miriam Cunningham Burney, first came to American Beach in 1936 as honeymooners. Mr. Burney was an executive in the Atlanta office of the Afro-American Life Insurance Company when American Beach was founded and developed. Through transfers and promotions, the Burney family came to the Afro's home office in Jacksonville. They built a family cottage on the northernmost end of American Beach. Mr. Burney also served as president of the Afro. This is an old favorite from the Burney collection.

Boiled Tongue

I. H. BURNEY

1 beef tongue
1 bay leaf
1 medium onion
1 carrot

1 celery rib, including leaves
½ cup white vinegar
Salt and pepper

Wash tongue thoroughly. Place in a 5-quart Dutch oven and cover completely with water. Add the rest of the ingredients and bring to a boil. Lower heat and simmer for 2 to 3 hours, until tongue is tender.

Remove tongue from pot. When it becomes cool enough to handle, peel away the skin. Refrigerate, slice, and serve cold with a cocktail sauce and garnishes such as pearl onions, marinated baby carrots, or grape tomatoes. Serves 8.

Spinach Balls

MARSHA DEAN PHELTS

4 10-ounce packages frozen chopped spinach
4 cups packaged herb stuffing mix
2 large onions, diced
8 eggs
1 cup Parmesan cheese
1½ cups butter or margarine, melted
1 tablespoon ground thyme
2 garlic cloves, peeled and minced
Salt and pepper to taste

Cook spinach according to package directions and drain, squeezing liquid from the spinach. Mix the drained spinach with the rest of the ingredients and chill for 2 hours.

Roll the chilled mixture into 1-inch balls. Preheat oven to 300°. (You may freeze for later use.)

Bake 30 minutes, or until golden. Makes nearly 100 delicious treats.

Spinach Dip

MARSHA DEAN PHELTS

1 10-ounce box frozen chopped spinach, thawed, drained, and squeezed dry
½ cup minced parsley
3 shallots, minced
1 1.4 ounce package Knorr vegetable recipe mix
1 teaspoon bottled hot pepper sauce
1 tablespoon lemon juice
Salt and white pepper to taste
8 ounces whipped cream cheese
½ cup sour cream
½ cup mayonnaise

Place all ingredients except cream cheese, sour cream, and mayonnaise in a food processor fitted with the metal blade. Pulse a few times. Add cream cheese, sour cream, and mayonnaise and pulse a few times. Consistency should be that of a soft spread or dip. Cover and refrigerate until chilled. Serve with thick chips or seasoned croutons. Makes 1½ pints.

LaShonda Jewel Holloway created this recipe using the initials by which her friends address her: "LJ," for love and joy. LaShonda asserts that all food is tasty when made with love and served with joy.

Love and Joy Oyster Dip

LASHONDA JEWEL HOLLOWAY

1 3.6-ounce can smoked oysters
8 ounces cream cheese, softened
Worcestershire sauce
1 teaspoon prepared horseradish

Drain oil from oysters. Combine all ingredients with love, taking care to mix well. Shape mixture into a ball or block and chill until ready to serve. Enjoy with pita chips, wheat crackers, or julienned vegetables. Serves 6–8.

LaShonda Jewel Holloway with the Asparagus/Sprenger fern, which has been handed down by the Tunsil-Holloway family for seven generations.

Avocado Crab Dip

MARSHA DEAN PHELTS

1 large avocado, diced
8 ounces cream cheese, softened
¼ cup sour cream
1 tablespoon lemon juice
1 tablespoon grated onion
1 teaspoon Worcestershire sauce
¼ teaspoon monosodium glutamate, optional
¼ teaspoon salt
8 ounces crabmeat

Blend everything except the crabmeat. Add crabmeat and serve with assorted crackers. Makes 1½ pints.

Shrimp Dip

MARSHA DEAN PHELTS

2 4-ounce cans small shrimp
½ cup mayonnaise or sour cream
1 teaspoon grated onion
1 teaspoon lemon juice
1 teaspoon grated lemon rind

Drain shrimp and rinse in cold water. Mash with a fork. Add remaining ingredients and mix well. Add additional mayonnaise or sour cream to reach desired consistency. Chill and serve with chilled raw vegetables. May also be used as a sandwich spread. Serves 6–8.

Tipsy Shrimp Spread

MARSHA DEAN PHELTS

1½ pounds small cooked shrimp
1 cup rum
1 stick butter or margarine
1 tablespoon grated onion or onion juice
1 tablespoon lemon juice
1 teaspoon dry mustard
Salt and pepper to taste
½ teaspoon bottled hot pepper sauce
½ teaspoon Worcestershire sauce

Marinate cooked shrimp in rum for 1 hour. Drain. Grind shrimp in a meat grinder or food processor and combine with remaining ingredients. Chill and serve on bread squares or with potato chips. Serves 6–8.

My son, Kyle, prefers a pungent taste in his creative concoction. Much like me, Kyle has been cooking nearly all his life. During his childhood, we did a lot of backyard cooking. To this day, Kyle prefers the outdoor grill to cooking inside. He has worked in specialty restaurants in California and Florida. My husband, Mike, and I rely upon Kyle and his son, Kurt, year-round to assist us in beach cookouts.

Black Man's Ambrosia

KYLE DEAN

Wooden skewers
1 pound prawns (4–8 per pound) or very large shrimp
½ cup soy sauce
6 ounces of beer
½ slice of bacon per prawn

Soak wooden skewers in half can of beer to keep damp during grilling. Marinate prawns in soy sauce and the remaining half can of beer for 30 minutes in refrigerator.

Preheat grill.

To grill, wrap each prawn in a half bacon slice and thread onto a skewer. Place on a hot grill, 2½ minutes per side. Turn as needed.

Brush beer over bacon-wrapped prawn at each turn or as needed. Serves 4.

This is a black man's ambrosia, according to Kyle and his friends. They think of this as hors d'oeuvres straight from heaven.

My only child, Kyle Michael Dean, with actor Barbara Montgomery at the Isle of Eight Flags Shrimp Festival (1990). Montgomery lived on American Beach in the 1980s and the 1990s.

Red Deviled Spiced Shrimp and Sauce

MARSHA DEAN PHELTS

½ cup buttermilk (to make buttermilk, add 1 tablespoon white vinegar or lemon juice to 1 cup of milk and refrigerate 30 minutes)
2 eggs, slightly beaten
1 teaspoon bottled hot pepper sauce
½ teaspoon sea salt
1 teaspoon freshly ground white pepper, optional
2 pounds large shrimp, peeled and deveined, with tails intact (see shrimp section in chapter 11)
2 cups spicy brown mustard, such as French's, Gulden, Grey Poupon
2 cups self-rising flour
1 tablespoon paprika
Oil

Combine buttermilk, eggs, hot pepper sauce, salt, and pepper (if using) in a bowl; coat each shrimp with this mixture. Place mustard in another bowl and coat each shrimp with mustard. Mix flour with paprika and coat each shrimp.

Heat 3 inches of oil to 360° in a deep pan or use a deep fat fryer. Drop batches of shrimp into hot oil; do not crowd. Remove shrimp as soon as they brown and drain on paper towels. Serves 4–6.

Sauce:

¼ cup oil
½ cup minced onion
3 tablespoons chili sauce
1 clove garlic, peeled and crushed or grated
¾ teaspoon salt
1 tablespoon Worcestershire sauce
1 tablespoon prepared mustard
1 teaspoon bottled hot pepper sauce

Heat oil in a saucepan until hot but not smoking. Sauté onions and garlic in oil until soft but not brown. Add remaining ingredients and cook 3 minutes. Serve as a dipping sauce with 2 pounds of cooked shrimp or other seafood.

My husband, Michael, has been active in the kitchen for as many years as I have. When it comes to seasoning and frying seafood, he is hard to top. One fall weekend in 2000 we decided to go over to Savannah. Mike and his mother and sister rode the train, and I drove the car to pick them up at the station and to have transportation while there. We ventured all over the place, and it was a fulfilling retreat for each of us. We stumbled upon the smallest restaurant imaginable, but it drew us like the power of a magnet. There was a display case from which they serve golden brown crab balls the size of a small orange or large lemon. Mike didn't even ask the cook for the recipe. As he savored the flavors, he formulated his own way of creating these balls and even added shrimp to the mix.

Crab and Shrimp Poppers

MICHAEL PHELTS

1 pound claw crabmeat (Phillips or other good-quality)
1 medium onion, minced
1 medium red, yellow, or orange bell pepper, minced
½ pound medium shrimp, slightly cooked
1 package Old Bay Original Recipe Crab Cake Classic
½ cup mayonnaise
Juice of one lemon or lime
1 tablespoon Worcestershire sauce
1 egg, slightly beaten
Salt and white pepper
½ cup fine dry bread crumbs
1 tablespoon paprika
2 tablespoons cooking oil to sauté vegetables
1 cup cooking oil for frying Crap and Shrimp Poppers

Drain and remove any cartilage from crabmeat. Sauté onions and peppers for 5 minutes. Cut each shrimp in 3 or 4 pieces. Mix Old Bay with mayonnaise, lemon or lime juice, and Worcestershire sauce. Gently combine egg, sautéed vegetables, and shrimp in a large bowl and mix in the Old Bay mixture, salt and pepper to taste. Carefully add the crabmeat. Shape into 1½-inch balls. Mix paprika with bread crumbs and coat each ball. Refrigerate balls at least 1 hour, or until firm and seasonings are set. Preheat oven to 375°.

My husband, Michael (*left*), and his brothers, Gerald and Russell Phelts.

Bake balls for 15 minutes. Balls may also be fried quickly in deep fat until golden brown.

The choice to bake or fry is yours. If these little poppers frizzle and become crumbly while frying, the oil is too hot; if they fall apart while frying, the oil is too cold. Oil temperature should range between 350° and 375°. Don't ruin a one. Crab and shrimp poppers won't last long, as diners toss these morsels into their mouths one by one until they are all gone. They can be made ahead of time and kept in the freezer. Makes 30–36.

Pickled Shrimp

MARSHA DEAN PHELTS

½ cup celery leaves
¼ cup pickling spices
1 tablespoon salt
2 quarts water
3 pounds large fresh or frozen shrimp in the shell

2 cups sliced onion
7 bay leaves
1½ cups oil
¾ cup white vinegar
3 tablespoons capers and juice
2½ teaspoons celery seed
1½ teaspoons salt
Bottled hot pepper sauce

Add celery leaves, pickling spices, and salt to 2 quarts of water. Bring to a boil, add shrimp, and simmer until shrimp turn pink, no longer than 5 minutes. Drain immediately.

Peel and devein shrimp under cold running water. Alternate layers of shrimp, onion, and bay leaves in a large shallow dish. Combine oil, vinegar, capers and juice, celery seed, salt, and hot pepper sauce to taste. Mix well. Pour over layers. Cover and chill at least 24 hours, spooning marinade over shrimp occasionally.

When ready to serve, arrange on a bed of greens on a platter or use toothpicks to attach to a lettuce-covered 2½-foot Styrofoam cone. Anchor the cone securely to a 12-inch × 12-inch × 1-inch Styrofoam square as a base. Place the cone in the center of the Styrofoam square and draw a circle around the base of the cone. Cut out the circle and insert the cone. Cover the base and the cone with overlapping leaves of lettuce or Belgian endive. Start at the bottom of the base and work up the cone. Serves 24–30.

Crab Dabs

MARSHA DEAN PHELTS

1 12-ounce can Dungeness crabmeat, fresh or frozen
1 pound blue crabmeat
⅓ cup fine soft breadcrumbs
2 tablespoons dry sherry
1 teaspoon minced chives
1 teaspoon dry mustard
¼ teaspoon salt
10 slices bacon, cut in thirds
30 wooden toothpicks

Drain crabmeat and remove any shell or cartilage. Combine all ingredients except bacon and mix thoroughly. Chill for 30 minutes. Soak the toothpicks in water until ready to use.

Shape 1 tablespoon crab mixture into a small roll. Wrap a piece of bacon around the crab roll and secure with a water-soaked toothpick. Repeat until the crab mix is gone. Place crab rolls on a broiler pan. Broil about 4 inches from heat for 8 minutes, or until bacon is crisp. Turn carefully. Broil 4 minutes longer, or until bacon is crisp. Makes 30.

Aunt Liza's Sardine Supremes

ELIZA ROSIER GLASS

3 8-ounce packages cream cheese, softened
2 cans skinless or smoked sardines
1 teaspoon salt
2 tablespoons paprika
1 large onion, grated
½ cup capers, drained and minced
½ cup minced parsley
½ cup minced mint
Juice from ½ clove crushed garlic
1 tablespoon Worcestershire sauce
1 tablespoon bottled hot pepper sauce
1 tablespoon monosodium glutamate, optional
Grated peel from 1 large lemon
Juice of 1 lemon

Mix all ingredients well and place in a mold. Refrigerate overnight. Remove from mold onto a chilled platter and serve with hot cocktail biscuits. Serves 20.

Cheese Bites

MARSHA DEAN PHELTS

2 cups all-purpose flour
1 teaspoon salt
¼ teaspoon cayenne pepper
2 sticks butter or margarine, softened

2 cups grated sharp cheddar cheese
1 cup chopped walnuts or pecans
1 teaspoon baking powder

Sift flour, salt, baking powder, and cayenne together. Blend with butter or margarine in a bowl until smooth. Stir in cheese, then nuts, and mix until well blended. Divide mixture in half, forming each half into a roll 1 inch in diameter. Wrap rolls securely in plastic wrap. Refrigerate for an hour, or until firm. Preheat oven to 350°.

Cut rolls into ¼-inch slices and place 1 ½-inches apart on baking sheets.

Bake 10 to 15 minutes, or until centers are firm to the touch. Makes about 6 dozen.

Cheese Straws

MARSHA DEAN PHELTS

1½ cups grated sharp cheddar cheese
½ cup butter or margarine, softened
1½ cups all-purpose flour
1 teaspoon baking powder
½ teaspoon salt
1 teaspoon sugar
1 teaspoon cayenne pepper
   Preheat oven to 350°.

Mix cheese and butter in a bowl until smooth and light. Add all dry ingredients and mix until smooth. Pack this mixture in a cookie press fitted with the star plate and squeeze out 2-inch-long ropes on an ungreased cookie sheet. Bake for 15 minutes, or until cheese straws begin to brown. Makes approximately 2 dozen.

Cheese Crisps

DELORIS GILYARD

2 sticks butter or margarine
2 cups all-purpose flour
2 cups grated sharp cheddar cheese

1 tablespoon cayenne pepper
2 cups crisped rice cereal
   Preheat oven to 350°.

Cut butter into flour until it looks like coarse meal. Add cheese and mix well. Add cayenne pepper and cereal and mix well. Shape into 1-inch balls and place on an ungreased cookie sheet. Mash balls with a fork.
   Bake for 15 minutes. Makes approximately 48.

Cheese Puffs

MARSHA DEAN PHELTS

2 cups grated cheddar cheese
2 teaspoons Worcestershire sauce
1 teaspoon paprika
1 teaspoon dry mustard
4 egg whites, beaten stiff
White sandwich bread

Remove crusts from bread slices and cut into 1-inch squares or cubes.
   Mix cheese, Worcestershire sauce, paprika, and mustard. Fold in beaten egg whites. Dip or cover bread in mixture and broil until cheese puffs. Serve hot. Serves 30. This is a popular treat.

These recipes for deviled eggs are a part of this cookbook because of the distinct flavor of each of these delicious party staples.

Petronella's Crab-stuffed Eggs

ALMA GREENE

12 hard-boiled eggs
1 cup crabmeat
1 cup finely chopped celery
2 tablespoons finely chopped green bell pepper
½ cup sour cream
1 tablespoon dry Italian salad dressing mix
Salt, pepper, and bottled hot pepper sauce to taste
Paprika

Peel eggs and cut in half. Remove yolks and combine with crabmeat, celery, bell pepper, sour cream, salad dressing mix, salt, pepper, and hot sauce. Stuff the egg whites with the mixture and sprinkle with paprika. Serve on a chilled egg platter. Makes 24.

Southern-style Deviled Eggs

EVELYN JONES

1 dozen eggs
1 cup mayonnaise
½ teaspoon Emeril's Fish Rub
½ teaspoon Morton Nature's Seasons® Seasoning Blend
¼ teaspoon sugar
Paprika, pimentos, sliced olives

Hard boil eggs. Place cooked eggs in a bowl of cool water until cool enough to peel. Peel carefully to keep from breaking the white of the egg. Cut peeled eggs in half lengthwise, separating the yolk from the white.

Evelyn Jones, a year-round resident, and her big brother, Aaron Jones Jr. Both are Nassau County natives (1946).

Place white halves on a dish (preferably a deviled-egg dish) and the yolks in a bowl. Mash the yolks until smooth, add the remaining ingredients, and mix well.

Fill a cake-decorating tube (a plastic sandwich bag with a corner nipped will serve just as well) with the yolk mixture and fill each egg white. Sprinkle each deviled egg with paprika or garnish with pimentos or sliced olives. Makes 24.

Tomato Pizza

MARSHA DEAN PHELTS

1 loaf white sandwich bread
1 pound cheddar cheese spread
4 plum tomatoes, thinly sliced
1 pound onions, thinly sliced
Catsup

Remove crusts from bread and quarter each slice. Spread bread squares with cheese, a thin slice of tomato and onion, and a plop (1 teaspoon) of catsup.

Broil 4 to 5 inches from heat until cheese melts. Makes 80–100.

Peppered Pecans

MARSHA DEAN PHELTS

3 tablespoons butter or margarine
½ teaspoon garlic powder
1½ teaspoon bottled hot pepper sauce
½ teaspoon seasoned salt
3 cups pecan halves

Heat oven to 250°.

Melt butter or margarine and stir in seasonings. Place pecans in a single layer in a 9-inch × 13-inch baking dish. Spoon butter or margarine over pecans and stir to coat. Bake, uncovered, 1 hour, or until pecans are crisp, stirring every 20 minutes. Remove pecans from oven and cool to room temperature. Store in airtight containers, gift tins, or zipper-top bags at room temperature for up to one month. Serves 10–12.

Glazed Nuts

CONGRESSWOMAN CORRINE BROWN

¼ cup orange juice
¼ teaspoon grated lemon peel
1 cup sugar
2 cups pecan halves

Combine orange juice, lemon peel, and sugar; mix well in a glass or microwave-safe pan. Add nuts and coat well.

Cook for 5 minutes on 70% power in a microwave oven with a revolving turntable. Stir and cook 5 minutes more at same setting.

Remove from microwave and spread on wax paper to harden. Do not let nuts cluster. Serves 8. This recipe makes the most delicious candied pecans.

Congresswoman Corrine Brown at the baptism of my only granddaughter, Kayaunna Rinders Dean, with Canon Nelson Pinder.

4

Salads

Ambrosia
Cranberry Salad
Cornbread Salad
Island Fruit Salad
Grilled Fruit Salad with Yogurt
Fruit Salad
Crustacean Cocktail Salad
Christmas Pea Salad
Confetti Salad
Green Derby Special House Salad
Spinach Salad
Garden Salad
Aunt Liza's Cottage Cheese Salad
Deviled Tomatoes
Emma's Pole Bean Salad

There is nothing to compete with Florida oranges but Florida oranges.

HENRY FLAGLER

S weet, fleshy Florida navel oranges stir up fond memories of the Christmases of my childhood. The Christmas season continues to be a joyous and exciting time for me. Big Mama's (Mama's mama's) annual Christmas dinner began with the serving of ambrosia. Simple, sweet, and so good ambrosia. Florida navel oranges peak during the winter holidays and are the main ingredient. I shake with thrills thinking of these lush sections of fruit from God.

Look for Florida oranges in your grocery store or produce stands. If Florida navel oranges are not available in your region, it is worth the money to send off for a mail order supply for the Christmas season. Try and get your Florida friends or relatives to send you a bushel. The shipping may cost more than the oranges, but, oh, what a treat! I have not yet experienced an orange that equals a navel orange grown in Florida.

There are three ways to get the most from a Florida navel orange. Eat it straight from the peel, make ambrosia, or bake an orange pie. Don't forget! The key is that the oranges are grown in Florida soil. Florida produces a far superior quality when it comes to oranges and mangos.

Big Mama, Agnes Cobb, established treasured family traditions that keep her alive in our hearts.

Ambrosia

AGNES LLOYD COBB

6 Florida navel oranges, #1 grade
1 cup shredded coconut, fresh or dried

Peel and cut the white membrane from the oranges. Remove the membrane from each orange section. In a crystal compote bowl alternate layers of orange sections and long shredded coconut. Chill until serving time. Serves 6.

This is all that we use to make ambrosia—oranges and coconut—period. If you need to add sugar to sweeten the ambrosia, you've got the wrong oranges.

If you must make ambrosia without Florida navel oranges, then I recommend that you add sugar and anything else you desire in a fruit salad.

Cranberry Salad

MARSHA DEAN PHELTS

1 small package cherry-flavored gelatin
1 envelope unflavored gelatin
½ pound fresh cranberries
1 navel or seeded orange, chopped, or 1 cup mandarin orange slices
Juice of 1 lemon
1 cup finely chopped celery
1 cup finely chopped pecans or walnuts

Make cherry-flavored gelatin and plain gelatin according to package directions, mix together, and refrigerate. Cook cranberries in boiling water to cover for 5 minutes and drain. In a blender mix cranberries with orange, lemon juice, celery, and nuts. Refrigerate the blended fruit mixture in separate container for one hour while gelatin thickens.

Stir the drained cranberry, fruit, and nut mixture into the jelled mixture, pour into a mold, and refrigerate until firm. Serves 8.

Serve as a tasty condiment with game, fish, or poultry. Once you make this recipe you won't buy canned cranberries again.

Cornbread Salad

TERRI SINGLETARY AND CHERYL L. WRIGHT

1 package corn muffin mix
1 cup minced green bell pepper
1 cup minced sweet onions
½ cup sweet pickle relish
3 cups diced tomatoes
12 slices crisp bacon, crumbled
1 cup mayonnaise
¼–½ cup sweet pickle juice
Red, yellow, and orange bell pepper, minced, for garnish

Prepare corn muffin mix as directed on package. Crumble cooled cornbread in a bowl and set aside; reserve a few tablespoons for topping. In a medium bowl, mix bell peppers, onions, relish, tomatoes, and bacon, and set aside. In another bowl, mix mayonnaise and pickle juice until you have a creamy dressing.

In a large serving bowl, place a layer of cornbread, then a layer of bell pepper mix, then a layer of the mayonnaise dressing. Repeat until all the bell pepper mixture is used, ending with a layer of the mayonnaise dressing. Garnish with crumbled cornbread and minced bell pepper. Serves 8.

Dennis Stewart, a.k.a. Mr. Natural, is a welcome sight at any function. This highly acclaimed local chef is known for swiftly swinging his blades and utensils with precision. He is an artistic and culinary whiz when it comes to preparation and presentation. Known for using fresh and natural ingredients, Mr. Natural can be found providing his specialized services at every special occasion from the Virgo Bash on American Beach to special and holiday presentations at the Ritz-Carlton on Amelia Island. Mr. Natural's cooking can be seen on Martha Stewart's show and has been taste-tested by thousands at fishing tournaments, jazz festivals, and the games of the Jacksonville Jaguars.

Dennis Stewart, Sr. and Jr., celebrating July 4, 1948—where else but American Beach.

Island Fruit Salad

DENNIS STEWART (MR. NATURAL)

½ pint strawberries
1 small cantaloupe, halved
1 pineapple, halved
1 banana, sliced
1 mango
1 navel orange

1 small papaya
Juice of ½ lime
Freshly ground nutmeg
Kiwi, sliced, for garnish
Mint, for garnish

Peel all the fruits except the cantaloupe, pineapple, and strawberries. Remove all seeds. Dice cantaloupe and pineapple into bite-sized pieces after removing fruit from rinds.

Combine fruits and lime juice; sprinkle lightly with nutmeg. Serve in cantaloupe or pineapple rinds for decorative island flair. Garnish with kiwi slices and/or mint. Serves 6.

Grilled Fruit Salad with Yogurt

DENNIS STEWART (MR. NATURAL)

Ingredients:

Apples, mangos, pineapple, and pears (fruits such as strawberries, bananas, peaches, cantaloupe, papaya, and honeydew are also flavorful when grilled, but be careful not to burn them—they cook faster than harder fruits)

Citrus Bath:

Juice of 1 fresh orange
Pinches of ground cinnamon, freshly ground nutmeg, and ground ginger
1 teaspoon firmly packed light brown sugar

Yogurt Dressing:

1 tablespoon raw honey
1 pinch each ground cinnamon and freshly ground nutmeg
8 ounces vanilla yogurt
1 teaspoon vanilla extract

Preheat grill.

Cut the fruit in half, leaving the skin on, and remove any seeds or pits. Combine all ingredients for citrus bath and dip the fruit in it. Place fruit, skin side up, over a medium fire for approximately 5 minutes, or until golden brown and grill marks can be seen. (Bananas are done as soon as the peel of their skin turns black.) Remove from grill, cool, remove skin, and cut fruit into chunks.

Combine all ingredients for yogurt dressing and toss with fruit. Eight ounces of dressing is enough for 4 cups of fruit. Serves 8.

Fruit Salad

MARSHA DEAN PHELTS

2 cups orange sections
2 cups pineapple chunks
1 cup red maraschino cherries
1 cup maraschino green cherries

3 cups fresh sliced peaches
2 cups flaked coconut
2 cups apple chunks
2 cups banana chunks
½ cup sliced fresh ginger
1 cup sour cream
1 cup mayonnaise
1 cup whipped cream

Mix all ingredients except the whipped cream. Fold in the whipped cream, cover tightly, and chill 3 hours before serving. Serves 8–10.

Crustacean Cocktail Salad

FRANCES AND GEORGE GREEN

1 pound large shrimp, peeled and deveined, tails intact
1 tablespoon of Old Bay Seasoning
1 package crab and shrimp boil
1 medium bell pepper (any color), diced
4 scallions, minced
2 celery ribs, diced
⅓ cup sweet pickle relish
2 hard-boiled eggs, peeled and minced
½ cup mayonnaise
½ cup sour cream
1 pound jumbo or lump crabmeat
3 lemons, sliced in wedges
Lettuce leaves

Place shrimp in water seasoned with Old Bay or any Crab and Shrimp Boil Seasoning water and cook for a few minutes until they turn pink. Cool by adding ice cubes to the cooking water to stop cooking and to allow the shrimp to absorb the seasonings.

Mix the bell pepper, scallions, and celery with the hard-boiled eggs, mayonnaise, and sour cream. Fold in the crabmeat, being careful not to shred it. Cover tightly and refrigerate while preparing the shrimp. When ready to serve, place a large scoop of crab salad in the middle of a lettuce leaf and garnish with a few shrimp and a lemon wedge. Serves 4–5.

George Green, once baby of the family, is now the patriarch of a one-time large Franklin Town family.

Christmas Pea Salad

MARSHA DEAN PHELTS

1 15-ounce can of red beans
1 15-ounce can of black beans
1 15-ounce can of green pigeon peas
6 green onions, minced
6 sprigs parsley, minced
1 bottle raspberry walnut vinaigrette
3 hard-boiled eggs, peeled and sliced, for garnish

Drain and rinse the beans and peas. Place in a mixing bowl with green onions and parsley and mix well. Pour raspberry walnut vinaigrette over the vegetables, cover, and refrigerate overnight. Serve on a bed of lettuce or mixed salad greens and garnish with egg slices. Serves 12–16.

Confetti Salad

SARA HEATH

1 16-ounce can French-style green beans, drained
1 12-ounce can shoe peg corn, drained

1 17-ounce can green peas, drained
1 cup diced celery
1 bunch green onions, thinly sliced
1 green bell pepper, minced
1 2-ounce jar diced pimentos, drained

Note: The can size isn't too important, and any other vegetables you have on hand can be substituted. However, I highly recommend that you get shoe peg corn. The texture and flavor of this corn adds to the appeal of this dish.

Marinade:

1 cup sugar
¾ cup apple cider vinegar
½ cup oil
1 tablespoon water
1 teaspoon salt
1 teaspoon pepper

Combine the vegetables. Prepare the marinade by combining all ingredients in a saucepan and bringing to a boil. Stir until sugar is dissolved. Cool completely. Pour marinade over vegetables, cover, and chill for at least 8 hours, stirring occasionally. Serves 10–12.

This recipe results in the tastiest green salad I've ever eaten. The Green Derby's special house salad can be a meal in itself. The Green Derby was an acclaimed Jacksonville steak house.

Green Derby Special House Salad

2 tablespoons olive oil
2 tablespoons wine vinegar
Salt and pepper to taste
¼ teaspoon monosodium glutamate, optional
¼ teaspoon ground oregano
1 tomato, quartered
⅓ head lettuce, cut (or torn) into 1½-inch pieces
3 tablespoons minced parsley
1 tablespoon minced scallions

Syrian bread, toasted and cut in 1-inch squares
2 tablespoons freshly grated Parmesan cheese

For two salads: Measure into a large wooden salad bowl 2 tablespoons olive oil and 2 tablespoons wine vinegar. Add salt and pepper to taste, monosodium glutamate (if using), and oregano. Add 3 tomato quarters and chop into dressing mixture. Add the cut lettuce, parsley, and scallions. Add toasted croutons and toss lightly. Transfer to individual salad bowls and sprinkle each with 1 tablespoon Parmesan cheese. Salad must be served immediately. Serves 2.

Spinach Salad

MARSHA DEAN PHELTS

1 pound fresh spinach
½ pound fresh bean sprouts
1 can sliced water chestnuts, drained
6 slices cooked, crumbled bacon, or 4 tablespoons bacon bits
3 hard-boiled eggs, peeled and sliced

Dressing:

⅔ cup sugar
⅓ cup catsup
1 tablespoon Worcestershire sauce
1 teaspoon salt
¼ cup cider vinegar
1 cup olive oil

Combine vegetables, bacon or bacon bits, and hard-boiled eggs. Prepare dressing by combining all ingredients and mixing well. Serves 4–6.

Garden Salad

CLARETHEA EDWARDS BROOKS

1 head romaine lettuce, cut or torn into bite-sized pieces
½ cup crumbled feta cheese
3 green onions, minced
½ cup sliced carrots

½ cup canned sliced beets
2 hard-boiled eggs, peeled and sliced, for garnish

Toss all ingredients in a large bowl and serve with your favorite salad dressing. Serves 4–6.

Aunt Liza's Cottage Cheese Salad

ELIZA ROSIER GLASS

1 small package lime-flavored
    gelatin
1 cup boiling water
1 cup crushed pineapple, drained

1 cup cottage cheese
½ cup mayonnaise
½ cup canned evaporated milk
½ cup pecans or walnuts

Dissolve gelatin in boiling water; add pineapple and cottage cheese. Stir in the remaining ingredients, mix well, and refrigerate. Serves 6.

Deviled Tomatoes

MARSHA DEAN PHELTS

6 plum tomatoes
1 16-ounce package frozen baby peas, thawed
6 scallions, minced
6 sprigs parsley, minced
6 slices bacon, fried crisp and crumbled
6 slices water chestnuts, minced
1 tablespoon prepared horseradish
3 hard-boiled eggs, peeled and minced
½ cup mayonnaise
¼ cup sour cream
Salt and freshly ground white pepper
Bottled hot pepper sauce to taste

Cut tomatoes in half lengthwise. Remove pulp and seeds, leaving a shell. Save tomato pulp for use in vegetable soup or some other dish. In a bowl mix remaining ingredients and spoon into tomato shells. Refrigerate stuffed tomatoes until completely chilled. Serves 12.

    Deviled tomatoes may be beautifully arranged on a deviled egg platter.

Emma's Pole Bean Salad

EMMA HOLLEY MORGAN

1 pound fresh Florida pole beans
1 cup diced celery
2 tablespoons minced green onion
1½ cups julienned deli style
   lunch meat
½ cup mayonnaise

1½ tablespoons vinegar
1 teaspoon dry Italian salad
   dressing mix
Salt and pepper to taste
Garlic powder to taste
Lettuce and sliced tomato, for garnish

Wash pole beans and remove ends. Cut beans crosswise into 1-inch pieces. Cook beans uncovered in boiling salted water to cover for 5 minutes. Cover pot and continue cooking beans 10 minutes. Remove beans and plunge into cold water to stop the cooking. Drain.

    Combine celery, onions, and lunch meat in a serving bowl with pole beans. Combine remaining ingredients and toss with pole beans. Garnish dish with lettuce and sliced tomatoes if you choose. Serves 4–6.

American Beach was a hot spot in 1960. From left, Annie Holley Carlise, Emma Holley Morgan, Carrie Johnson, Gloria Anderson Finch, and Sylvia Johnson (the little girl).

5

Super Bold Sandwiches

Fishwich
Viola's Veggiewich
Eggplant Sandwich
Leftover Shrimp Sandwich
Leftover Liver Sandwich
Peanut Butter and Honey Raisin Sandwich
Cucumber Sandwiches
Fried Tomato and Cream Cheese Sandwich
Sandwich Platter

He may do it with a better grace, but I do it more natural.
WILLIAM SHAKESPEARE

Throughout Florida, rustic restaurants at fish camps are noted for serving fresh and delicious seafood. At shanty crab houses, diners take delight in raking crab, oyster, and clam shells and table scrapings through the center of the tables into trash receptacles underneath.

The Rev. William "Bill" Holmes's paternal grandmother, "Miss Lizzie" Simmons, owned a restaurant at the port of Fernandina on the Amelia River. Stories continue to circulate about the restaurant she owned and operated at the foot of Centre Street. Miss Lizzie's restaurant was built over the river. When customers placed orders for a fish sandwich or dinner, a trap door in the floor of the kitchen was opened. Miss Lizzie sprinkled a handful of fish bait in the water and whatever fish came to the surface first was what the customer was served. Hot, fresh, fried fish.

Although there are only a limited number of sandwiches in this chapter, I have included them because I want sandwich lovers to experience the same ecstasies I do when the right applications come together for a midday meal. For me these "super bold sandwiches" represent the genius of presenting everyday food another way.

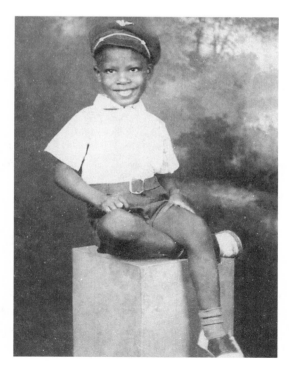

Bill Holmes grew up around the port of Fernandina in a section of the city known as Old Town (1945).

The vegetable sandwiches are included because they satisfy hearty appetites. The meat sandwiches came about as a result of leftovers, which taste even better a day or two later.

The way to come by a fishwich is to cook the meat away from the carcass of a big fish. All the meat that can't be cut away from the bone can surely be cooked off the bone, which is how the fishwich found its way on our menus. These sandwiches use the part of these large fish that is too good to throw away or feed to the cats.

Fishwich

MARSHA DEAN PHELTS

½ onion, minced
½ green bell pepper, minced
½ pound drum- or white fish
½ pound salmon
½ pound grouper
½ cup fresh bread crumbs
2 tablespoons Worcestershire sauce
Juice of 1 lemon or lime
2 eggs, beaten
½ cup mayonnaise
1 tablespoon bottled hot pepper sauce
1 teaspoon white or black pepper
Salt to taste
2 tablespoons olive oil
Additional bread crumbs for dredging

Sauté onion and peppers in olive oil until soft but not brown. Steam the three fish types until they begin to flake easily with a fork and lose the translucent or raw appearance. Flake the fish and mix with bell pepper and onion. Sprinkle in bread crumbs and fold in the remaining ingredients (except bread crumbs for dredging), being careful to keep the fish in lumpy flakes. Shape into 6 big burgers. Coat by lightly spooning breadcrumbs over fish cakes. Cover and refrigerate for an hour so the cakes will hold together and the seasonings will set in.

Heat the olive oil until hot but not smoking. Pan fry the fishwiches in hot oil until brown on both sides. Serve on the best bun you can buy with your choice of trimmings, such as lettuce, tomatoes, pickles, and onion slices. Spread the bun with mayonnaise, mustard, or horseradish sauce. The only way you will know just how good a fishwich is, is to try it for yourself. Serves 6.

~

This creation came to American Beach when Viola Walker of Detroit relocated there in 2000. This sandwich is a novel approach to blending fresh vegetables in an exotic medley of tidbits. These sandwiches are as in demand as her fried whiting sandwiches.

American Beach resident Viola Walker and her neighbor Ron Miller at Evans' Rendezvous.

Viola's Veggiewich

VIOLA WALKER

2 large whole wheat pita breads
1 head romaine lettuce (or your choice of salad greens)
1 bell pepper, any color, sliced into strips
8 ounces bean sprouts
1 Spanish or Vidalia onion, sliced
2 beefsteak tomatoes, sliced
4 slices cheddar cheese (or your choice)

Sliced sandwich dill pickles

¼ cup salad dressing (e.g., Miracle Whip; don't use mayonnaise because heating will break it down)

Preheat oven to 400°.

Cut pita breads in half and separate to form two pockets from each round. Separate lettuce enough for two medium leaves per sandwich. Line insides of pita pockets with salad dressing. Stuff each pita with lettuce, pepper strips, bean sprouts, two or more slices of onion, tomatoes, cheese, and sandwich dills. Wrap each sandwich snugly in aluminum foil and bake for 15 minutes. Do not overcook. The vegetables should remain firm. Serves 4.

Lisa Harter makes her sandwiches with homemade, hand-sliced bread. Her delicious eggplant sandwich is a popular item with diners at La Bodega Courtyard Café in the historic district of downtown Fernandina and easy to duplicate at home.

Eggplant Sandwich

LISA HARTER

1 garlic clove, peeled and sliced
¼ cup extra-virgin olive oil
1 medium eggplant, unpeeled, cut in ½-inch slices
Rustic white bread
Goat cheese
Mixed salad greens

Preheat oven to 350°.

Marinate garlic slices in olive oil for 30 minutes.

Lightly coat both sides of eggplant slices with garlic-flavored olive oil and roast for 25 minutes. Serve on homemade rustic white bread with goat cheese and mixed salad greens. Serves 4–6.

Leftover Shrimp Sandwich

MARSHA DEAN PHELTS

Fresh spinach leaves or salad greens of your choice
4 slices wheat bread
3 tomatoes, thinly sliced
1 scallion, minced
1 dozen leftover pickled shrimp (see p. 55)

Place spinach or salad greens on one side of 2 slices of bread, followed by tomato and scallion. Divide the pickled shrimp between the other two slices of bread. Put the sandwich together, slice in half, and enjoy the creation. Serves 4.

My daddy's favorite sandwich for lunch was icebox-cold leftover beef liver. When the liver was hot it was a dinner meal.

My daddy, Charles Rosier Sr. (1933).

Leftover Liver Sandwich

CHARLES ROSIER SR.

1 pound beef liver, sliced (approximately 4 slices)
Salt and pepper
½ cup all-purpose flour
1 large onion, sliced
¼ cup oil
Catsup
Onions, sliced

Peel the membrane from liver slices. Season liver with salt and pepper to taste. Dredge each slice in flour. Heat the oil in a frying pan until hot but not smoking. Fry sliced onions until tender. Remove the onions from the pan and fry liver over medium-high until juices begin to appear on top; turn and fry other side until brown, around 6 minutes.

For a cold sandwich, cut liver in half to fit on sandwich bread. Spread 2 tablespoons catsup on bread; add two cold liver slices and onions if you have any for a delicious sandwich. A hot liver sandwich pales in comparison to a leftover cold one. The cold sandwich is firmer and handles better. Serves 4.

My mama, Eva Cobb Rosier (1933).

Mama used to make these sandwiches for us (in the late 1940s), when we were still too little to make them for ourselves. Peanut butter and honey raisin remains her favorite sandwich filling, and she continues to make them for an evening snack.

Peanut Butter and Honey Raisin Sandwich

EVA R. LAMAR

1 cup peanut butter
½ cup honey
⅓ cup seedless raisins
Pumpernickel bread

Mix the peanut butter, honey, and raisins in a bowl until smooth. Spread on pumpernickel sandwich bread. Makes 1 cup.

Cucumber Sandwiches

MARSHA DEAN PHELTS

8 ounces cream cheese, room temperature
½ cup sour cream
½ teaspoon dried dill weed
1 teaspoon salt
1 good-sized cucumber, ¼ peeled and diced, ¾ sliced into ⅛- –¼-inch rounds
Cocktail rye bread or white sandwich bread
Dried dill weed, for garnish

Mix the cream cheese, sour cream, dill weed, and salt until well blended. Blend the diced cucumber into the cream cheese mixture and let stand for at least 15 minutes to allow the flavors to blend.

If cocktail rye bread is used, the bread may be untrimmed. If using white bread, trim the crusts and cut into desired shapes. Use white bread that has some body to it, at least a day or two old. You will find that bread from the bakery is better than that found on the grocery shelves for this recipe.

Spread about a tablespoon of cream cheese mixture on each slice of bread. Top with a slice of cucumber and sprinkle with a pinch of dill. Makes 30.

Fried Tomato and Cream Cheese Sandwich

MARSHA DEAN PHELTS

1 clove garlic, peeled and minced
¼ cup minced parsley
⅛ teaspoon salt
1 teaspoon minced fresh basil
8 ounces cream cheese, softened
4 firm beefsteak tomatoes, each cut into 3 ½-inch thick slices
½ cup all-purpose flour
1 egg beaten with 1 tablespoon milk
⅔ cup dry breadcrumbs
3 tablespoons olive oil
3 tablespoons butter or margarine
Fresh basil or parsley, for garnish

In a mixer or food processor combine the garlic, parsley, salt, basil, and cream cheese. Spread 6 tomato slices with 2 tablespoons of cream cheese mixture; top with remaining slices to make 6 sandwiches. Dredge each in flour, then in egg mixture, and finally in crumbs.

Heat olive oil and butter in a frying pan until hot but not smoking. Fry tomato sandwiches over medium heat until brown on both sides. Garnish with fresh basil or parsley. Serves 6.

Sandwich Platter

MARSHA DEAN PHELTS

Order a pullman loaf of bread from the bakery in a major grocery store. Have them color the bread; red works beautifully for me. Have the baker hand slice the loaf horizontally three times to get 4 slices.

You will need three fillings for this sandwich loaf. Have the fillings ready when you begin to create your sandwich loaf platter.
1 pound ham, chicken, or red salmon salad
1 pound egg salad made from 6–8 eggs
1 6-ounce package bean or broccoli sprouts or 2 cups shredded lettuce (wash and dry greens and coat with 2 tablespoons olive oil)
¾ cup mayonnaise
3 8-ounce packages cream cheese, softened

8 ounces sour cream

2 tablespoons minced fresh dill

Carefully remove the sliced loaf from the bag and keep the layers in order. Begin construction of the sandwich from the bottom.

Spread mayonnaise on inside of bottom layer, then spread on the meat or fish salad. Spread mayonnaise on bottom side of the next slice and place over the meat layer. Spread mayonnaise on top of that slice and then spread the egg salad on this slice. Spread mayonnaise on the bottom of the next bread slice and place over the egg salad layer. Spread mayonnaise on top of that slice and add the sprouts or lettuce. Spread the inside of the top layer of bread with mayonnaise and cover the sandwich. Wrap the sandwich snugly so it will hold its shape and refrigerate for a minimum of 3 hours.

After the sandwich has been refrigerated, mix the cream cheese and sour cream well. Spread the softened cream cheese mixture all over the Pullman loaf except the bottom. It will look like a loaf cake. Scatter or sprinkle minced dill or any other garnish over the covered loaf. Rewrap the loaf and refrigerate 3 hours.

You may prepare the fillings beforehand, but make this mouthwatering sandwich on the day that you intend to serve it. Just allow yourself enough time to refrigerate in between construction. Slice with an electric knife and serve to a ravenous group. Serves 20.

6

Vegetables

Stewed Eggplant
Ratatouille
Eggplant Baked with Ham and Tomato Sauce
Squash and Eggplant Casserole
Squash Casserole
Down–home Fried Squash, Corn, and Okra
Corn Pudding
Corn and Tomatoes
Broccoli Supreme
Vegetable Paella
Mashed Turnips
Collard Greens
Beets
Beets in Orange Sauce
Carrot–Orange Soufflé
Mrs. Mary's Cheesy Tomato Pie
Macaroni and Cheese Casserole
Fresh Vegetable Rice
Mrs. Morgan's Rice Dressing

*As a hard-working farmer, let me tell you, the farming life
leaves precious few hours for anything but simple cooking.*

DORI SANDERS

The first time Emma Holley set eyes on the Atlantic shores it was from American Beach. Emma visited during the summer of 1945 with a group of students from Tuskegee Institute. They stayed in the oceanfront home of Tuskegee alumna Elizabeth Cobb, an RN at the veterans' hospital.

Emma remembers how Ms. Cobb assembled the students to witness A. L. Lewis's visit to the beach. Word quickly spread of his visit. Mr. Lewis's entourage arrived in a fleet of black luxury cars. First out was the chauffeur. Following the chauffeur were the maids and then the helpers. Next, the family members made their exits from the cars. Finally, the grand old man himself, Mr. A. L. Lewis, stepped from his limousine.

People stood gazing from afar and from as near as they dared. Ms. Cobb's home was next door to the Lewises, and while they gathered on her lawn he waved to cheering crowds that lined the streets and lawns, and all was well.

There were many other memories that the Eufaula, Alabama, college student would keep from that visit. Emma Holley experienced her first restaurant meal at Lee's Ocean View Inn. This was the establishment where Mary McLeod Bethune vacationed while visiting American Beach.

Beautiful shells from the sea served as centerpieces on the tables. Emma, a home economics major, gathered a box of seashells and a bag of

Frank Morgan takes Emma Holley to be his bride on December 20, 1958.

beach sand for keepsakes. For her home management class at Tuskegee, Emma used the shell collection to design a most beautiful arrangement using shells, sand, model people, and trees. She received an A for it.

In 1948 Emma came back to Jacksonville, where she was employed by the Cooking and Baking School for Veterans. Years later she would meet Frank Morgan of Thibodeaux, Louisiana. They were married in 1958, and the Morgans' fondest dream—owning a home on American Beach—became a reality when Ms. Cobb sold the young couple her home the summer of 1960.

Stewed Eggplant

EMMA HOLLEY MORGAN

4 tablespoons butter or margarine
1 large onion, minced
1 green bell pepper, minced
1 28-ounce can chopped stewed tomatoes
1 teaspoon dried basil
Salt and pepper
1 large eggplant, peeled and diced
¾ cup grated cheddar cheese
¼ cup grated Parmesan cheese
1 cup croutons

Preheat oven to 350°.

Heat the oil until hot but not smoking. Sauté onion in butter until soft; add bell pepper and cook until soft. Add stewed tomatoes and mix well. Salt and pepper to taste. Add eggplant, cover, and simmer for 10 minutes.

Remove from heat, fold in the cheddar cheese and Parmesan cheese. Top with croutons and bake until bubbly, approximately 30 minutes. Serves 6.

~

For over fifty years, ratatouille has been among Gwen Leapheart's standby vegetable entrées, which she takes pride in serving. Ratatouille is a French recipe blending eggplant with other summer vegetables and can be served hot or cold. Long before she built a beach house, Gwen, who has traveled around the globe, came to American Beach for recreation. For years she

Florida's American Beach (Nassau County) and Manhattan Beach (Duval County) pioneer families enjoy the night at Small's on Broadway (circa 1950s). From left, "Little" Jackie Davis, organist; Gwen Leapheart; and the Wilson siblings, Elaine, Maxie, and Frances.

and her mother, Netty, visited beaches all along the East Coast; however, American Beach remained their favorite beach spot.

After retiring from a career in civil service in New York, Gwen returned to Jacksonville, where her support remained solid through the years, and became the first woman elected to the Jacksonville Civil Service Board in 1977. Gwen is active in religious, civic, and social circles, so demands on her hospitality keep her on the go making special arrangements for one function after another. Yet she manages to keep an impressive calendar and, with an abundance of charisma and hospitality, entertain friends. Gwen is highly praised for her culinary skills, and on American Beach, guests enjoy eating ratatouille and other treats that she prepares. For ratatouille, she combines a succulent assortment of young garden-fresh vegetables that release stimulating flavors.

Ratatouille

GWENDOLYN LEAPHEART

3 tablespoons olive oil
2 medium onions, sliced
2 cloves garlic, peeled and minced
2 tomatoes, peeled and diced
1 large green bell pepper, cut into ½-inch strips
1 eggplant, unpeeled and diced
2 small zucchini, cut in ½-inch slices
1 bay leaf
3 slices bacon, optional
2 teaspoons salt
⅛ teaspoon pepper

Heat oil until hot but not smoking in a Dutch oven. Sauté onions with garlic until tender. Add tomatoes, bell pepper, eggplant, zucchini, and bay leaf; sauté over medium heat, stirring occasionally, 15 minutes.

Meanwhile, cook bacon until crisp. Remove from the pan with a slotted spoon, drain on paper towels, and crumble; add to vegetables with salt and pepper. Cover; simmer 15 minutes. Uncover; simmer 10 minutes. Remove bay leaf. Serve hot or cold. Serves 6.

Eggplant Baked with Ham and Tomato Sauce

METRO SMITH GRIFFITH

2 medium-sized eggplants, peeled and cut into ⅓-inch thick slices
Salt
3 cups tomato sauce
2 teaspoons fennel powder
3 cloves garlic, peeled and crushed
3 tablespoons extra virgin olive oil
2 cups ground ham
1 pound of sliced mozzarella cheese
1 cup Parmesan cheese

Preheat the oven to 350°.

Salt both sides of each eggplant slice and let them drain, or soak them in salted water ½ hour. Wipe them dry with paper towels.

Mix the tomato sauce with the fennel powder and crushed garlic. Heat the olive oil until hot but not smoking. Sauté the eggplant until tender. As the eggplant is done, layer it in a 9-inch × 13-inch baking dish, covering each layer with tomato sauce, ground ham, thin slices of mozzarella cheese, and a sprinkle of Parmesan cheese. Cover the top with the remaining Parmesan cheese. Bake 20 minutes. Serves 8.

Squash and Eggplant Casserole

DOLORES PONDER SHAW

3 zucchini, sliced	1 teaspoon salt
2 yellow squash, sliced	1 tablespoon mayonnaise
1 medium eggplant, peeled and cubed	2 cans minced clams, drained
	1 egg, beaten
1 can white cream sauce	Parmesan cheese
1 tablespoon butter or margarine	1 cup fresh or dried breadcrumbs

Preheat oven to 325°.

Cover zucchini, yellow squash, and eggplant with salted water in a saucepan, bring to a boil, lower the heat, and simmer over medium heat until tender. Drain and combine with remaining ingredients, except Parmesan cheese and breadcrumbs, in a large bowl. Spread mixture in a greased 9-inch × 13-inch casserole and sprinkle with Parmesan cheese and breadcrumbs. Bake for 30 minutes. Serves 6.

Squash Casserole

LOIS ISZARD

8 or 10 medium yellow summer squash, sliced
¼ cup minced green bell pepper
½ cup minced onion
4 tablespoons butter or margarine
½ cup mayonnaise
1 egg, beaten
1 tablespoon sugar
1 4-ounce jar pimentos, minced
¼ cup grated sharp cheese
Salt and pepper

Preheat oven to 350°.

Add squash, bell pepper, onion, salt, and pepper to boiling water and simmer until tender. Drain and add butter or margarine, mayonnaise, egg, sugar, and pimentos. Place in greased 9-inch × 13-inch casserole and top with grated cheese. Bake for 30 minutes. Serves 6.

~

Dorothy Patrick says, "This original recipe was passed down from my grandmother in South Carolina. The recipe has been reduced in quantity: it originally served eleven children and two adults."

Down-home Fried Squash, Corn, and Okra

DOROTHY PATRICK

2 medium yellow squash, sliced ¼ inch thick
1 medium zucchini, sliced ¼ inch thin
1 large yellow onion, sliced thin
1 medium green bell pepper, sliced thin
8 ounces okra, sliced ½ inch thick (may use frozen)
3 ears fresh corn, kernels removed from cob (may substitute 10-ounce box frozen or 15¼-ounce canned)
4 tablespoons oil
Salt and pepper to taste
1 tablespoon ground oregano, optional
1 teaspoon dried basil, optional
½ teaspoon garlic powder, optional
1 large, firm tomato, coarsely chopped

Combine all vegetables except the tomato in a large bowl. Heat oil in large frying pan until very hot but not smoking. Add vegetables and stir until well coated. When vegetables begin to brown, cover pan and reduce heat. Cook for 15 minutes, stirring occasionally, or until tender. Add the chopped tomato during the last 2 minutes of cooking. Do not overcook. Serve as a side dish or over rice. Serves 6.

Corn Pudding

MARSHA DEAN PHELTS

6 slices bacon
1 green bell pepper, minced
½ cup minced onion
4 tablespoons bacon fat, butter, or margarine, divided
4 cups fresh, frozen, or canned corn
4 tablespoons all-purpose flour
Salt and pepper
¼ teaspoon ground nutmeg
½ teaspoon turmeric, optional
4 tablespoons oil, divided
½ cup milk
1 cup light cream
3 eggs, beaten

Preheat oven to 325°.

Cook bacon until crisp, drain on paper towels, and crumble. Sauté bell pepper and onion in 4 tablespoons butter, margarine, or bacon fat until tender. Stir in corn, flour, salt and pepper to taste, nutmeg, turmeric (if using), and 3 tablespoons oil. Add milk and cream.

Grease a 9-inch × 13-inch casserole with remaining tablespoon of oil. Pour mixture into casserole and sprinkle bacon on top. Bake for 1 hour. Serves 8–10.

Corn and Tomatoes

EUGENE K. EMORY

¼ cup minced onions
3 tablespoons butter or margarine
1 cup fresh bread crumbs
2 cups corn kernels
3 large tomatoes, seeded and sliced ¼ inch thick
Salt and pepper
¾ cup light cream, optional

Preheat oven to 350°.

Heat butter or margarine until hot but not smoking. Sauté onion until soft. Stir in bread crumbs and cook until crumbs are golden. In a 2½–quart baking dish, layer half the corn, half the tomatoes, and half the crumb mixture; salt and pepper to taste. Repeat. Pour cream over the top, if desired. Bake for 40 minutes. Serves 6.

Broccoli Supreme

LOIS ISZARD

1 medium onion, minced
1 stick butter or margarine
2 10-ounce packages frozen broccoli, cooked according to package directions and drained
1 roll garlic-flavored cheese
1 small can sliced mushrooms
1 can mushroom soup
1 cup shredded cheddar cheese, optional

Preheat oven to 350°.

Heat butter or margarine until hot but not smoking. Sauté onions until soft but not brown. Add all other ingredients except cheese. Top with cheese, if using. Bake for 25 to 30 minutes. Serves 6.

Vegetable Paella

BELVA BURNEY PETTIFORD

3 tablespoons olive oil
2 onions, thinly sliced
4 small green bell peppers, thinly sliced
1 large tomato, diced
1 clove garlic, peeled and minced
2 cups rice
4 cups water, divided
1 bay leaf
1 teaspoon saffron
Salt
1½ cups canned green peas, drained
Pimento, for garnish

Heat olive oil in a large pot until hot but not smoking and sauté onions, bell peppers, tomato, and garlic until soft. Set aside. Cook rice, covered, in 2 cups water until water is absorbed. Mix rice with sautéed vegetables, add remaining water, bay leaf, saffron, and salt to taste. Cover and cook over very low heat until water is nearly absorbed and rice is tender, approximately 20 minutes. Carefully blend in peas and cook 1 minute more. Garnish with pimento. Serves 4.

Mashed Turnips

DOROTHY PATRICK

3 pounds turnips
1 stick butter or margarine

¼ cup cream
Salt and pepper

Wash turnips well and place in a Dutch oven. Cover with water, bring to a boil, and cook uncovered for 45 minutes, or until turnips are tender. Drain. When turnips are cool enough to handle, peel and mash with a potato masher until smooth. Add butter, cream, and salt and pepper to taste and whip or beat until blended. Serve piping hot. Serves 6.

Throughout the Southland, the cooking and serving of a vegetable commonly known as greens is a welcome treat on the dinner menu year-round. Most people do a noble job in seasoning and cooking this popular green leafy vegetable whether they cook it half a day or half an hour. My husband cooks greens no less than once a week. His recipe is a common way of preparing them and is included for the novice at cooking greens. A variety of greens are available to choose from, such as collards, turnip greens, mustard greens, kale, and poke salad. The key to their flavor and taste lies in the seasoning, which is as varied as the greens. Greens are cultivated in gardens, available at the markets or grocers, and grow free and wild.

Collard Greens

MICHAEL PHELTS

1 large bunch collard greens
1 pound chicken backs
Salt and pepper

Oil
2 cups water
1 medium whole onion

Wash greens and cut into small pieces. Season chicken backs with a little salt and pepper. Heat oil to a depth of 2 to 3 inches until hot but not smoking. Brown the chicken backs lightly and put into a large pot with the water. Place the greens and onion into the pot and bring to boil. Lower heat and simmer the greens for 2 hours. Serves 6.

Beets

The eating of fresh-cooked beets is an unusual experience for many. I treasure finding fresh beets in the produce department. A bunch consists of 3 to 4 beet roots attached to the leaves and serves 2. They must be washed thoroughly. It takes no time to cook up their leaves, which are tender, cook as quickly as spinach, and have a similar taste. Beetroots take from 1½ to 2 hours to cook.

I boil beets in a pot of water and add only my teeth to them once they are done and their skins are peeled off.

If you can't find fresh beets, this recipe will greatly improve the flavor of canned beets.

My husband, Michael, on graduation day, Edward Waters College, with Aunt Corrie Weeks and Michael's little brother and sister, Stephen and Carol Phelts (1967).

Beets in Orange Sauce

MARSHA DEAN PHELTS

2 tablespoons cornstarch
2 tablespoons beet juice or water
1 cup orange juice
4 tablespoons lemon juice
2 tablespoons white vinegar
2 tablespoons sugar
½ teaspoon salt
2 #2 cans baby beets
4 tablespoons butter or margarine
2 tablespoons grated orange peel

Mix cornstarch with beet juice or water and add to orange juice, lemon juice, and vinegar. Cook over low heat until clear. Add sugar, salt, and beets. Heat until beets are warm, then stir in butter or margarine and grated orange peel. Serve hot. Serves 4–6.

I was four or five years old in this picture. It was a great joy to be able to eat tomatoes and sweet potatoes straight from our garden.

Carrot-Orange Soufflé

METRO SMITH GRIFFITH

2 cups mashed carrots (7 new carrots)
2 tablespoons honey
¼ teaspoon ground mace or nutmeg
Salt and pepper
1 tablespoon grated orange rind
4 tablespoons minced green or white onion
½ cup orange juice
4 tablespoons cornstarch
⅓ cup orange juice
Juice of ½ lemon
4 egg yolks, beaten
4 egg whites, stiffly beaten

Preheat oven to 350°.

Trim and scrub the carrots, mince, and put in a heavy pot with the honey, mace or nutmeg, salt and pepper to taste, orange rind, onion, and the ½ cup orange juice. Cover tightly, bring to a boil, lower heat, and simmer 15 minutes until they are done. Press the carrots through a sieve or purée in a food processor.

Blend the cornstarch with the ⅓ cup of orange juice and the lemon juice. Cook over low heat until thick. Slowly add some of the carrot mixture to keep it from thickening too much. Blend the rest of the carrots with the cornstarch mixture and let cool. Then add the beaten egg yolks. Stir in one-fourth of the whites, then lightly fold in the rest. Bake in a greased 8-inch soufflé dish 25 minutes. Serves 6.

Mrs. Mary Stewart lives on Amelia Island in Stewartville, a half mile north of American Beach. Stewartville is so named because the full-time residents of this African American enclave are members of the Stewart family. Mrs. Mary is a welcome sight driving her blue pickup truck around the neighborhood. She drives all over the south end of Amelia Island picking up aluminum cans and other items for recycling. While making her daily rounds, she drops off at various houses ripe tomatoes and produce that vendors give her. Mrs. Mary learned to bake tomato pies from her grandmother Rainey Moore when they were living in Pensaw, Alabama, during the Depression.

Mrs. Mary's Cheesy Tomato Pie

MARY STEWART

1 unbaked 10-inch pie shell
2 large ripe tomatoes, cut into
   ½-inch slices
Salt and pepper
⅓ cup all-purpose flour
2 tablespoons olive oil
1 cup sliced green onions, divided

½ cup sliced olives
3 slices provolone cheese
2 eggs, slightly beaten
1 cup shredded cheddar cheese
1 cup canned evaporated milk
2 tablespoons cornstarch

Preheat oven to 350°.

Prick the bottom and sides of the pie shell and bake 8 minutes. Cool. Increase oven temperature to 375°.

Sprinkle the tomato slices with salt and pepper to taste and dredge in flour; shake off excess flour. Heat the olive oil in a pan until hot but not smoking. Sauté the tomato slices until golden brown. Set aside 2 tablespoons onions; sprinkle the remaining onions and olives evenly in the cooled pastry shell. Top with provolone cheese and tomato slices.

Combine the eggs and shredded cheddar cheese with the evaporated milk, cornstarch and mix well. Pour over the tomatoes. Bake 40 minutes, or until set. Top the pie with the reserved onions and let sit a few minutes before serving. Serves 8.

Macaroni and Cheese Casserole

COMILLA BUSH

8 ounces macaroni
1 4-ounce can mushroom stems and pieces
1 16-ounce jar Alfredo Sauce
½ pound sharp cheddar cheese, cut in chunks
4 tablespoons butter or margarine, divided
Paprika
Salt and pepper to taste

Preheat oven to 325°.

Boil macaroni in two quarts salted water for 20 minutes; drain. Place half of macaroni in a buttered 9-inch × 12-inch casserole dish. Sprinkle with mushroom pieces and cover with remaining macaroni. Stir cheese chunks into Alfredo sauce and pour mixture over macaroni and mushrooms. Add salt and pepper as needed. Sprinkle paprika evenly over mixture, dot with remaining butter or margarine, and bake for 35 minutes, until bubbling. Serves 6.

Fresh Vegetable Rice

LOIS ISZARD

1 large sweet onion, sliced into thin rings
1 large carrot, sliced diagonally ¼ inch thick
1 celery rib, sliced diagonally ¼ inch thick
2 tablespoons butter or margarine
1 13¾-ounce can chicken broth
¼ teaspoon dried thyme
1½ cups instant rice

Heat butter or margarine in a large skillet until hot but not smoking. Sauté onion, carrot, and celery until tender but not browned, about 5 minutes. Add chicken broth and thyme and bring to a full boil. Stir in rice, cover, remove from heat, and let stand 5 minutes. Fluff with a fork before serving. Serves 4–6.

Mrs. Morgan's Rice Dressing

EMMA HOLLEY MORGAN

2 quarts water
1 pound chicken gizzards
⅛ teaspoon dried thyme
½ teaspoon dried sage
4 bay leaves
½ pound chicken livers
 (about 8 good-sized livers)
2 cups rice
½ pound ground beef
½ pound ground pork sausage
4 sticks unsalted butter

4 cups all-purpose flour
4 onions, minced
4 ribs celery, thinly sliced
4 green bell peppers, minced
Salt and pepper
1 teaspoon browning and seasoning
 sauce (e.g., Kitchen Bouquet)
1 clove garlic, peeled and minced
1 bunch scallions (6–8), minced
10–12 sprigs parsley, minced

Bring water to a boil, add gizzards, thyme, sage, and bay leaves, lower heat, and simmer for 1 hour, or until meat is tender. Add chicken livers in the last 5 minutes of cooking. Drain, reserving cooking water, and chop gizzards and livers.

Return 1 quart of the cooking water to a boil, add the rice, and cook, covered, over very low heat until rice is tender and water is absorbed, about 20 minutes. Set aside.

Season ground beef and pork sausage with salt and pepper to taste, thyme, sage, and bay leaves then brown over medium heat in an iron frying pan or a heavy pot. Combine with cooked rice and set aside.

Melt the butter in a 12-quart stockpot. Whisk in the flour and cook until foamy. Continue to cook, stirring often, until flour turns dark mahogany, about 1 hour. These are good instructions for making a roux, I just don't stay with it an hour. This recipe is very forgiving and I believe that it will come out well for a novice.

Preheat oven to 300°.

Add onions, celery, bell pepper, salt and pepper to taste, seasoning sauce, chopped giblets and livers, and any remaining liquid from giblets to the stockpot and continue to cook over low heat to make a thick gravy. Stir this gravy into the rice and meat mixture and bake for 20 minutes. Remove from oven and top with scallions and parsley. This is an incredibly delicious dish. Serves 8–10.

Mrs. Morgan takes a stand and makes a statement about the American Beach land.

7

Ice Potatoes

Southern Shrimp Potato Salad
German Potao Salad
Stewed Potatoes
Stuffed New Potatoes
Sinful Potatoes
Hash Brown Casserole
Margaret's Pride

*What I say is that, if a fellow really likes potatoes,
he must be a pretty decent sort of fellow.*

A. A. MILNE

W hile I was growing up, white or Irish potatoes were known as ice potatoes. Now, I have no idea why they were called ice potatoes. I can only suppose that it was because, as they were peeled and diced for potato salad, they were dropped in a bowl of ice water to prevent them from discoloring.

Beatrice Carter was an entrepreneur who operated a women's hosiery shop in black Jacksonville's LaVilla neighborhood on Davis Street, next to the Ritz Theatre (now the Ritz Museum and LaVilla Museum). She was known widely for her potato salad. Potato salad was as much a staple in picnic baskets as white bread, mustard, and hot sauce for a fish sandwich. Before World War II ended, Ms. Bea's family became early investors in American Beach. They had a cottage built and brought in an Airstream trailer. Family and friends by the hundreds took turns enjoying the Carter family's hospitality.

Over the years Ms. Bea's daughter, Francina, helped prepare beach fare for their guests. She improved upon her mother's traditional potato salad recipe by spiking the dish with succulent shrimp and sprinklings of savory spices. For years, people on the First Coast have placed orders with her for this recipe, which she now shares for *The American Beach Cookbook*.

American Beach and Franklin Town early residents. Top row, from left, Louise Sheffield and Francina King. Bottom row, from left, Beatrice Carter (Francina King's mother), Janie Madry, and Evelyn Jefferson.

Southern Shrimp Potato Salad

FRANCINA CARTER KING

8 medium or 2½ pounds of russet potatoes
½ cup minced scallions
4 hard-boiled eggs, peeled and minced
1 tablespoon celery seed
1 dash Old Bay Seasoning
¾ cup mayonnaise
1 dash seasoned salt
1 dash black pepper
¼ cup fresh chopped dill weed
½ teaspoon garlic powder
2 pounds medium shrimp, peeled and deveined
1 package crawfish, crab, and shrimp boil

Peel potatoes. Cover with salted cold water by 2 inches in a 3-quart pan and simmer uncovered until tender (not mushy), about 15 to 20 minutes. Transfer potatoes to a bowl of ice water. After potatoes have cooled, cut into cubes and place in a large bowl.

Combine potatoes, green onions, hard-boiled eggs, celery seed, Old Bay Seasoning, mayonnaise, seasoned salt, pepper, dill weed, and garlic powder and mix with a large fork.

Cook shrimp in crawfish, crab, and shrimp boil according to package directions, 2 to 3 minutes. Let shrimp cool, then add to potato salad and mix. Refrigerate for a short while. Serves 10.

German Potato Salad

MARSHA DEAN PHELTS

2 pounds small white potatoes, unpeeled
6 slices thick bacon
¾ cup minced onion, divided
1½ teaspoons all-purpose flour
4 teaspoons sugar
1 teaspoon salt
¼ teaspoon pepper
⅓ cup white vinegar
½ cup water
1 teaspoon celery seed
2 tablespoons minced parsley
½ cup thinly sliced radishes
Celery leaves

Cover potatoes with salted cold water by 2 inches in a 3-quart pan and simmer uncovered until tender, about 15 to 20 minutes. Drain, peel, and cut potatoes into ¼-inch cubes. Keep warm.

Cook bacon until crisp. Remove from the pan with a slotted spoon (reserve drippings), drain on paper towels, and crumble. Add ½ cup of the onions to the drippings and sauté until tender but not brown. Stir in crumbled bacon.

Mix flour, sugar, salt, and pepper in a bowl. Stir in vinegar and water and mix until smooth. Add the mixture to sautéed onions and crumbled bacon and simmer until slightly thickened.

Pour the hot mixture over the warm potatoes. Add remaining onions, celery seed, parsley, and radishes. Garnish with celery leaves. Serves 4–6.

~

Jeanette Mobley's family raises its own produce. This family has been cooking commercially on American Beach and Amelia Island for over a half century. On holidays and at reunions they begin the day with stewed potatoes. The family grew up on this and continues the tradition of eating this dish for breakfast on special occasions no matter where they live.

Stewed Potatoes

JEANETTE MOBLEY

4 strips bacon or salt pork
1 medium onion, diced
4 tablespoons all-purpose flour

2 cups water
6 potatoes, peeled and diced
Salt and pepper

Cook bacon until crisp. Remove from the pan with a slotted spoon (reserve drippings), drain on paper towels, and crumble. Sauté onions in the bacon drippings until soft but not brown, then stir in flour and brown to make a dark roux. Add the 2 cups water, potatoes, salt and pepper to taste, and bacon. Cover pan and cook down over low heat, approximately 15 minutes. Serves 4–6.

Stuffed New Potatoes

LOIS ISZARD

20 red-skinned new potatoes
2 medium-sized ribs celery, cut in ⅛-inch dice

2 scallions, cut in quarters lengthwise, then in ⅛-inch dice
1 medium carrot, cut into ⅛-inch dice
2 hard-boiled eggs, peeled and coarsely grated
2 tablespoons finely minced sweet gherkins
4 tablespoons finely chopped fresh dill, divided
2 tablespoons minced Italian parsley
¾ teaspoon coarsely ground black pepper
½ teaspoon salt
1 cup mayonnaise
1 cup sour cream

Drop whole potatoes into a large pot of boiling water and cook for 12 to 15 minutes, until tender. Drain. When potatoes are cool enough to handle, cut in half. Cut a tiny slice off the bottom of each half so it will stand upright. With a small scoop or melon baller, carefully scoop out the center of each potato half, leaving a strong potato shell. Place potato centers in a bowl and reserve the shells. Gently toss potato centers with celery, scallions, carrots, eggs, gherkins, 2 tablespoons dill, parsley, pepper and salt.

Combine mayonnaise and sour cream and gently fold into the potato salad with a rubber spatula. Adjust seasoning. With a small spoon, carefully mound salad inside the potato shells.

Refrigerate, covered, until serving. To serve, sprinkle with 2 tablespoons dill and arrange on a decorative platter or in a flat basket. Makes 40.

Sinful Potatoes

CHARLOTTE WOODS BURWELL

6 slices bacon
2 pounds frozen hash brown potatoes
16 ounces processed cheese (e.g., Velveeta)
2 cups Hellmann's mayonnaise (do not substitute)

Preheat oven to 350°.

Cook bacon until crisp. Remove from the pan with a slotted spoon, drain on paper towels, and crumble.

Put potatoes in 9-inch × 12-inch baking pan. Melt the cheese in the microwave. Mix mayonnaise and cheese together. Pour over potatoes. Mix well and spread potato and cheese mixture evenly in the pan. Spread crumbled bacon evenly over top. Bake uncovered 1 hour. Serves 6–8.

Hash Brown Casserole

2 pounds frozen hash brown potatoes
1 stick margarine
1 pint sour cream
1 can cream of chicken soup
2 cups grated sharp cheddar cheese
¾ cup minced onion

Thaw potatoes 30 minutes in a colander, to drain liquid.
Preheat oven to 350°.

Melt margarine in a 9-inch × 13-inch roasting pan and stir in the rest of the ingredients. Bake for 45 minutes. Serves 8.

Margaret Bennett Peyton brings this dish to family gatherings on the beach. As it sits on a long counter among seafood morsels, pans of barbecued meats, and favorite vegetables, diners take only a scant spoonful—in order to be polite. Yet Margaret's pride is the first dish to go because, after the first two bites, people rush back to get hearty lumps of it. Latecomers only get to hear about it.

Margaret's Pride

MARGARET BENNETT PEYTON

2-pound roll of sausage, hot or mild
32 ounces frozen hash brown potatoes
1 cup sour cream
½ red bell pepper
1 cup minced onions
1 can cream of chicken soup
1 8-ounce package French onion soup mix
1 8-ounce package grated sharp cheddar cheese

Preheat oven to 350°. Spray a 9-inch × 13-inch casserole dish lightly with nonstick spray.

Cook sausage until brown; drain. Mix all ingredients except sausage. Alternate layers of potato mixture and sausage in the casserole. Top with grated cheese and bake for 45 minutes. Serves 8–10.

8

Sweet Potatoes

Sweet Potato Pone
Sweet Potato Soufflé
Sweet Potato Cream Cheese Pie
Sweet Potato Boats
Candied Sweet Potatoes
Sweet Potato Pudding
Mommo's Sweet Potato Pudding

I still love their wonderful taste, and whenever I cook with them, I recall those childhood days of planting and harvesting and the sweet smell of the oakwood smoke coming from the sweet potato houses.

DORI SANDERS

y Big Mama Agnes Cobb's recipe is probably as old as the dirt that the first sweet potato grew in. To an aged southerner, sweet potato pone is the quintessential manner of offering homage to the winter holidays. Sweet potato pone is rich, and once you've tasted it, the desire for more will linger forever and ever.

Marjorie Kinnan Rawlings, who won the Pulitzer Prize in 1939 for *The Yearling*, implies in *Cross Creek Cookery* that sweet potato pone is a dessert enjoyed by poor southern folk. Having eaten this specialty treat my entire life, I can attest to its gourmet qualities.

There is nothing poor about sweet potato pone, however, not even the dirt that the sweet potatoes grew in. This dish is worthy of being served on New Year's Eve at Ritz-Carltons across the globe.

Grating enough sweet potatoes for a family gathering is hard work, but this dessert is worth every grated finger scrape that you mix in with the potatoes. Not a fiber of flavor is lost in grating the potatoes. Nature's sweetness is slow baked and sealed in the grated potatoes. Please try this recipe; let it become a part of your favorite family-gathering dishes. With food processors, the grueling task of hand grating is an agony of the past. I, however, continue to grate the potatoes by hand, for it is my only passage to succulent sweet potato pone.

Sweet Potato Pone

BIG MAMA AGNES COBB

4 cups raw grated sweet potatoes
2 cups firmly packed light brown
    sugar
1 cup maple syrup
4 eggs, well beaten
2 cups milk or cream

2 tablespoons butter, melted
1 teaspoon ground ginger
1 teaspoon grated orange rind
1 teaspoon ground cinnamon
1 teaspoon vanilla extract
1 teaspoon nutmeg

Preheat oven to 375°.

Grate the sweet potatoes. Stir in the sugar and syrup, eggs, milk or cream, melted butter, and spices, and pour into a well-greased deep iron frying pan or Dutch oven. Bake for 1 hour. If a toothpick inserted in the center comes out clean, the sweet potato pone is done. Serves 8.

This is a tasty and easy recipe to whip up. If you've prepared potato soufflé another way, give this recipe a try. You will be delighted with the flavors and crunchy toppings packed into this dish. After customizing this recipe to her creative culinary style, Barbara Jones finds herself making no fewer than forty soufflés for family and friends during the fall and winter holiday season. It is her husband, Carlton's, favorite.

Sweet Potato Soufflé

BARBARA GILLUM JONES

Soufflé:

3 cups cooked, mashed sweet potato
¾ cup sugar
3 eggs
1 tablespoon vanilla extract
½ cup canned evaporated milk
¼ cup butter or margarine, softened
Dash of salt

Special Topping:

1 cup firmly packed light brown sugar
½ cup self-rising flour
1 teaspoon ground cinnamon
1 cup chopped pecans
¼ cup butter or margarine, melted and cooled

Preheat oven to 350°.

For the soufflé, combine all of the ingredients in a large mixing bowl and beat at medium speed with an electric mixer until smooth, stopping several times to scrape the beaters and sides of the bowl. Spoon mixture into a greased 2-quart baking dish.

For special topping, combine brown sugar, flour, cinnamon, and pecans in a large mixing bowl. Stir with a spoon until uniform. Add melted butter or margarine and blend until moist and crumbly. Sprinkle evenly over the top of the potatoes and bake for 45 minutes, or until golden brown. Remove soufflé from oven and let it sit uncovered until ready to serve. Serves 6.

Sweet Potato Cream Cheese Pie

DOROTHY PATRICK

Sweet Potatoes:

2 large sweet potatoes, boiled
   whole in skin
1 stick butter or margarine
1 cup sugar
1 tablespoon ground cinnamon
1 teaspoon ground nutmeg
⅛ teaspoon ground cardamom

⅛ teaspoon ground ginger
1 can sweetened condensed milk
½ cup canned evaporated milk
3 eggs
¼ teaspoon grated orange rind
2 teaspoons vanilla extract

Peel sweet potatoes and mash while hot. Stir in butter or margarine, sugar, cinnamon, nutmeg, cardamom, ginger, condensed milk, and evaporated milk. Mix well with an electric mixer. Add eggs one at a time and mix after each addition. Stir in orange rind and vanilla. Set aside.

Cream Cheese Filling:

2 8-ounce packages cream cheese, softened
1 cup sugar
½ cup sour cream

It was love at first sight for New Yorker Dorothy Patrick and her family when they saw American Beach for the first time.

½ cup half-and-half
4 eggs
2 teaspoons vanilla extract
1 refrigerated piecrust

Preheat oven to 350°.

Beat cream cheese with an electric mixer until smooth. Add sugar and sour cream and mix until smooth. Add half-and-half and mix until incorporated. Add eggs one at a time, mixing after each addition. Stir in vanilla.

Lightly butter an 8 ½-inch × 12 ½-inch × 2-inch deep baking pan. Line pan with piecrust and pour potato filling over crust. Using a large spoon, ladle cream cheese filling carefully over surface of potato filling. Bake for 1 hour 15 minutes, or until knife inserted in center comes out clean. Remove from oven and cool. Can be served warm or chilled. Serves 6–8.

Sweet Potato Boats

EVELYN GREEN JEFFERSON

6 medium sweet potatoes
Oil
¼ cup molasses
¼ cup butter or margarine, melted
⅛ teaspoon ground nutmeg
¼ teaspoon ground cinnamon
¼ teaspoon salt
½ cup whipping cream

Preheat oven to 400°.

Wash potatoes well and rub with oil. Place on a baking sheet and bake for 1 hour, or until tender.
Raise oven temperature to 450°.

Cool potatoes, then slice the skin from the top of each potato lengthwise. Carefully scoop out the pulp, leaving shells intact. Combine sweet potato pulp, molasses, butter or margarine, nutmeg, cinnamon, salt, and whipping cream. Beat with an electric mixer until light and fluffy.

Spoon potato mixture into shells. Bake for 10 to 12 minutes, or until thoroughly heated. Serves 6.

Candied Sweet Potatoes

LARNEY OWENS

2 large sweet potatoes
1 large apple
2 slices fresh or canned pineapple
2 tablespoons firmly packed light brown sugar

Cook potatoes in boiling salted water to cover for 40 minutes, or until tender. Peel and quarter. Peel and core apple, halve, then cut each half crosswise into ½-inch slices. Halve pineapple slices. Reserve syrup from pineapple.

Arrange potatoes, apple, and pineapple in a broiler-proof 9-inch baking dish. Drizzle pineapple syrup over the dish, sprinkle with brown sugar, and broil 4 to 5 inches from heat for 15 minutes, or until apples are tender and starting to brown. Serves 4–6.

This old family favorite from I. H. Burney is the only canned sweet potato recipe that I received. It is included for when sweet potatoes are out of season or too pricey in the markets.

Sweet Potato Pudding

I. H. BURNEY

2 eggs
½ teaspoon ground cinnamon
¼ teaspoon ground nutmeg
½ #2½ can (3½ cups) sweet potatoes or yams, drained
3 tablespoons butter, divided
1 tablespoon lemon juice
1 teaspoon vanilla extract
½ cup firmly packed light brown sugar
1 tablespoon maple syrup

Preheat oven to 400°.

Whip eggs, cinnamon, and nutmeg together. Mash sweet potatoes or yams and combine with eggs. Melt the butter in a 2-quart casserole dish.

Add 2 tablespoons melted butter to the potato mixture, leaving 1 table-spoon in the dish. Pour sweet potato or yam mixture into the casserole dish and bake for 45 minutes. Serves 4.

Mommo's Sweet Potato Pudding

CAROL ALEXANDER

6 large sweet potatoes
1 stick melted butter
4 large eggs
1 teaspoon ground cinnamon
½ teaspoon ground nutmeg
1 teaspoon vanilla extract
1 tablespoon freshly grated orange peel, or 1 teaspoon dried
1½ cups sugar (use more sugar if potatoes are not at their peak)
½ cup half-and-half or cream
½ cup orange juice
Dash of salt
Butter for top of casserole

Preheat oven to 350°.
Boil sweet potatoes until tender. Peel and keep warm.
In a large bowl combine butter and hot sweet potatoes. Add eggs one at a time, mixing well after each addition. Add the remaining ingredients and stir until texture is smooth and loose. Pour the mixture into a well-greased 9-inch × 13-inch casserole or baking pan and dot with a few pats of butter. Bake for about 45 minutes. Serve hot as a side dish. Serves 6.

9

Seafood Secrets

Aunt Liza's Seafood Casserole

The ocean does not give up easily her secrets or her animals. Only by diligently searching will you learn where creatures spawn, what they eat, and where they hide.

JACK RUDLOW

I was seven years old when Aunt Liza allowed me to join her in the kitchen. Aunt Liza even designated the left front burner on her gas range as mine as I developed and practiced my cooking skills. I used leftover bits and pieces of meat, vegetables, or dough that she discarded to make my creations. In her small kitchen with its institution-sized stove, wall-to-wall floor-to-ceiling cabinets, and built-in cutting boards, Aunt Liza piped out a blend of aromas unlike any others I had known.

Because of her I acquired a taste for gourmet food long before I had the opportunity to eat in five-star restaurants or try my hand at preparing such fancy dishes. The warmth of Aunt Liza's kitchen made it my favorite place to be. I treasured standing by her side as she prepared food for special events such as the governor's inauguration, a debutante's party, or an enormous banquet. An aura of excitement permeated the home as she prepared for a party.

Our family had many occasions to visit Aunt Liza and Uncle Julius's home. Aunt Liza maintained a full and demanding schedule as a caterer, yet she managed to include quality time for family events and to take an annual vacation to attend the national convention of the Brotherhood of Sleeping Car Porters with Uncle Julius.

I am seven years old here (in this 1951 class photo), the little girl standing in the middle near the playhouse stirring the jar of paint. The teacher standing in front of the playhouse that my Uncle Scarborough built is Aunt Pearlie.

The Brotherhood of Sleeping Car Porters Convention in Washington, D.C. (1960). Uncle Julius Glass is seated to the far right. International president, A. Philip Randolph, is seated in the center. To the left of Randolph is Eastern zone supervisor Benjamin McLaurin. To the right of Randolph is international first vice-president Milton Webster.

Leading up to the Christmas holidays or shortly thereafter, Aunt Liza invited the whole family to dinner. We anticipated each feast. Their always beautiful home had a special appeal for me during the Christmas season, with its loads of prettily wrapped presents under a huge tree blanketed in tinsel, lights, and shiny glass ornaments.

Shortly after Christmas, Aunt Liza, who was my daddy's sister, recognized my birthday in January with gifts and treats just for me. Her thoughtfulness was very important to me because Mama and Daddy were slow to go all out with elaborate birthday plans right after Christmas.

Each year in February, my mama and I would dress up and go over to Aunt Liza's to have dinner with my hero, A. Philip Randolph. Mr. Randolph was the international president of the Brotherhood of Sleeping Car Porters. Under his leadership the porters became the first black labor union in the AFL-CIO. I was the only child in the crowd and felt privileged by this special invitation. The house was filled with excitement for me as well as other guests. Along with Mr. Randolph came the union's international vice-president, Mr. Milton Webster, and the Eastern zone director, Mr. Benjamin McLaurin.

Aunt Liza (1930).

Mr. McLaurin resided with Aunt Liza and Uncle Julius during the International Brotherhood of Sleeping Car Porters annual visit to Jacksonville, while Randolph and Webster were houseguests of Madame Alice Kirkpatrick in Jacksonville's exclusive Sugar Hill neighborhood. At these annual dinners during the 1950s and the 1960s, we spent the evening eating the finest foods served anyplace, listening to railroad and Pullman car stories from the East Coast of America to the West Coast, and playing a game of cards called dirty hearts.

The food that Aunt Liza served was fit for the king; however, it was the huge stainless steel pot filled with chitterlings rather than game hens or pineapple-glazed ham that was one of the favorite entrées. Even more prized than the chitterlings was the pièce de résistance: Aunt Liza's seafood casserole. Umph! Aunt Liza's seafood casserole is among my earliest memories of haute cuisine. Oh, the delicate morsels of lump crabmeat and chunky bites of lobster meat and succulent shrimp tossed with a pungent sauce resulted in divine dining!

While she worked as a caterer, Aunt Liza would not share her recipes with anyone, not even her siblings, on whom she called to work with her.

Aunt Liza often prepared seafood casserole for our family and for Mama's bridge club meetings; however, neither Mama nor Daddy, who was the youngest of the thirteen Rosier siblings, was ever provided with a recipe of Aunt Liza's.

To my amazement, when Aunt Liza died in 1974, she left me twelve ledgers of her catering engagements and recipes, which spanned a period from 1948 through 1972. The first recipe I tried was the seafood casserole, which, she noted, "is very special. Try it."

Since these recipes came into my possession, seafood casserole has become a favorite item on my Christmas dinner menu. When I prepare this enormous recipe, which serves twenty-eight, I give a casserole to my mama and another one to Aunt Liza's goddaughter, Congresswoman Corrine Brown, who grew up next door to Aunt Liza's taste-test kitchen. The rewards of sharing and having an extra dish to freeze for later use outweigh the cost. I make this only once a year. If you follow this recipe you will create an epicurean masterpiece that will elevate your culinary status. The only substitute I make is to use sea scallops in place of lobster meat. Please, make no substitutions for lump crabmeat. You must have this quality crabmeat for this casserole. Aunt Liza's shopping list in 1966 shows that lobster meat sold for $2.50 a pound; large shrimp, $1.10 per pound; and lump crabmeat at $3.00 a pound.

Aunt Liza's Seafood Casserole

1 green bell pepper, minced	3 tablespoons Worcestershire sauce
1 cup diced onion	1 teaspoon bottled hot pepper sauce
1½ cups diced celery	Salt
3 pounds lump crabmeat, cooked	1 4-ounce jar pimentos, minced
3½ pounds lobster meat, cooked	¼ cup lemon juice
3½ pounds large shrimp, cooked	Fine dry bread crumbs
10 eggs	Paprika
3½ cups mayonnaise	Water chestnuts, sliced , optional
8 tablespoons prepared mustard	

Preheat oven to 350°.

Steam bell pepper, onions, and celery until tender; drain. Combine with cooked seafood. Beat eggs until creamy; add mayonnaise. Beat until light and well blended, then add mustard, Worcestershire sauce, hot pepper sauce, and salt to taste. Picked crab meat comes cooked. To cook shrimp and lobster or scallops if used as a substitute for lobster, place each meat in an appropriate sized pot. Using 2 cups of tepid water to each pound of uncooked seafood. Season water with 2 tablespoons of a seafood seasoning such as Old Bay. Place seafood in pot and bring to a slight boil. As soon as shrimp and lobster turn pink and as scallops loose its raw sheen and turns opaque remove pot from heat for the seafood is done within 3 to 5 minutes. Drain. Pour this sauce mixture over the cooked seafood and vegetable mixture. Add the pimentos and lemon juice and mix with the fingers so as not to break up the seafood. Place the seafood mixture in a buttered 9-inch × 13-inch casserole dish or individual molds or shells; top with bread crumbs and paprika. Bake for 25 minutes. Serve at once. Sliced water chestnuts may be added atop the bread crumbs. Serves 28.

In Aunt Liza's ledger she also included the measures for tripling this recipe, as she frequently served this at dinner parties for 100 guests. This recipe can also easily be cut by one third. If the above recipe is cut by 1/3 it would serve 9. I am giving it to you straight from Aunt Liza's coveted workbook.

Several years ago my lifetime friend St. Frances Darby Daniels, asked me to prepare Aunt Liza's seafood casserole for a club that she would be entertaining. I was flattered and made the shopping list of ingredients that St. Frances needed. However, my friend asked that I purchase the items and bring her the bill, as I knew exactly what I needed. I immediately gave the list back to St. Frances and then wrote down the fish market and grocery store where she would find the best-quality ingredients. I absolutely refused to do the shopping. St. Frances couldn't understand why shopping was such an issue for me. Nevertheless, I flat-out refused to purchase the ingredients.

The Friday evening I walked in St. Frances's house to prepare the seafood casserole, she exclaimed, "Marsha! Now I see why you insisted I do my own shopping! You knew that I would not have believed the items would cost that much if I had not made these purchases myself." We burst into a hearty laugh, and I went right to work. The ladies and their guests had a perfect evening, and I left St. Frances with an extra seafood casserole to savor at her leisure.

Sometimes you just have to ignore the cost when you prepare for those you love. I don't believe that you will find a recipe as good as this one anywhere.

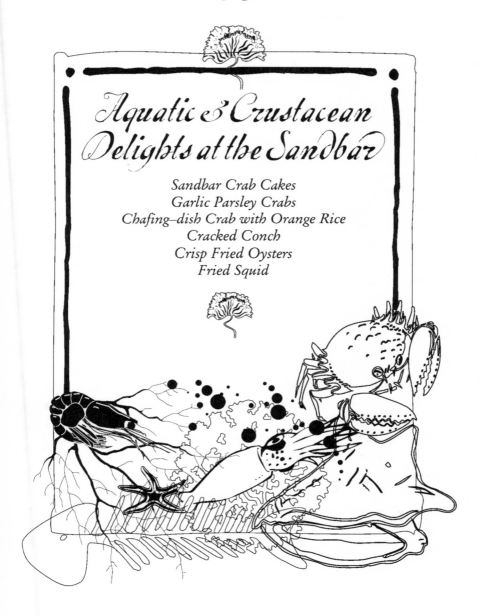

10

Aquatic & Crustacean Delights at the Sandbar

Sandbar Crab Cakes
Garlic Parsley Crabs
Chafing–dish Crab with Orange Rice
Cracked Conch
Crisp Fried Oysters
Fried Squid

Nestled under mammoth live oak trees on a bluff above the Intracoastal Waterway on Amelia Island, an island tradition endures!

JANINE CARLEY

The Sandbar was a family restaurant owned and operated by the family of Pierce and Lillie Johnson on the Amelia River. Its closing signified the end of an era.

The Sandbar began as a tavern in 1932 in the garage of the Johnsons' summer home. Deep in the forested south end of the island, this spot was far from the sight of prohibitionists. In compliance with the law, the Sandbar served wine and beer. It also served moonshine, which the owners called "near beer." Right away this tavern operating out of a converted garage became a popular drinking hideout. The Andrew Carnegies of nearby Cumberland Island frequented the Sandbar. Besides, there wasn't any law against ladies having drinks in taverns in the south end, although it was illegal in the City of Fernandina. Legends are rampant that Mrs. Carnegie had to drink sitting on a barrel on the sidewalk outside the Palace Saloon in town because it was against the law for ladies to be served at taverns in Fernandina.

For the sixty-three years that the Sandbar operated (1932–1995), the recipes for deviled crabs and crab cakes remained a highly guarded secret. Cook after cook mixed, shaped, and fried the deviled crabs and crab cakes, but outside of the family, no one knew the ingredients for the sauce that Lillian Johnson made in her home and walked over to the restaurant's kitchen daily.

I was able to pry this recipe from Elsie Manning Lohman, who was a preteen when she came to Amelia City with the Johnson family from Jacksonville as their live-in babysitter. After the Sandbar opened, Elsie became a cocktail waitress. The tavern soon became a seafood restaurant and bar.

On October 5, 1938, Elsie Manning became the bride of the Johnsons' neighbor, Rudolph Lohman. Their marriage took place in the priest's house of St. Joseph's Catholic Church in downtown Fernandina. In 1998 the Lohmans celebrated their sixtieth wedding anniversary with their four children.

Sandbar Crab Cakes

ELSIE MANNING LOHMAN

Sauce:

1 cup mayonnaise
6 teaspoons yellow mustard

2 teaspoons salt
1 teaspoon red pepper
¼ cup Worcestershire sauce

Mix ingredients for sauce together. The secret to the recipe is this sauce.

Crab Cakes:

2 tablespoons butter
1 small onion, minced
½ green bell pepper, minced
1 pound claw crabmeat
1 pound white crabmeat
1½ cups cooking oil
Cracker meal, as needed to hold ingredients together

Heat the butter in a saucepan until hot but not smoking. Sauté the onion and bell pepper until translucent. Combine the crabmeat, sautéed vegetables, and cracker meal, being careful not to break up the lumps of crab, and gently stir in the sauce. Shape into cakes or stuff mixture in crab shells. Fry cakes in enough cooking oil to half cover the cakes. If using crab shells, bake in 350° oven for approximately 20 minutes. Serves 10–12.

Follow this recipe exactly and you'll think that you are dining in the Tidewater region of the Chesapeake Bay.

Picked crabmeat is a costly luxury that you cannot afford to ruin. You must have the oil for frying at the right temperature; these crab cakes will hold their shape and are firm, golden brown crustacean morsels. If the oil is too hot the crab cakes tear up into crispy crumb strains. Just throw that away. If your crab cake breaks away when you get ready to turn it over then your oil is not hot enough and your crab cake will absorb too much oil. If you don't come up with a solid crab cake you've thrown away money. I have never used a cooking thermometer (or a double boiler), but 350° to 375° is a good temperature for frying fish, crabs, shrimp and other seafood. A rule of thumb is to fry until golden brown on both sides.

I cannot say enough about the merits of a well-seasoned iron frying pan. Do not overcook seafood. My preference is to deep-fry it, especially when I am cooking for more than two. Deep-frying is quicker and easier than pan frying because the food floats to the top of the oil when it is ready to be turned or taken out.

When I watch the skillful cooks on American Beach turn out scrumptious dishes, I realize that their timing isn't set by a thermometer but by skill. I can now buy a thermometer and a double boiler, but I'd most likely use them as much as I've used the vegetable steamer that I've left unopened for ten years.

~

A childhood friend, Roslyn Burrough, cooks by her senses rather than from a cookbook. Roz can create just about anything once she has tasted it. Some time ago (1993) a crab house in the area was selling its recipe for garlic crabs. Roz tasted the crabs but didn't buy the recipe; she decided to create her own. Roz bought crabs and seasonings, then drove down to the beach with everything but a government pot. While the crabs were bubbling in savory seasonings, she scribbled a recipe for garlic parsley crabs on the back of an envelope and left it with me. I've been cooking crabs this way for many years, to the delight of Low Country connoisseurs. Roz insists upon using butter rather than margarine.

Just Us, a group of lifelong friends. Seated, from left, Marsha Dean Phelts, Roslyn Burrough, and St. Frances Daniels. Standing, from left, Congresswoman Corrine Brown and Mildred Sapp.

Garlic Parsley Crabs

ROSLYN BURROUGH

2 dozen undressed crabs, steamed or boiled
Garlic powder, to taste
Lemon pepper, to taste

Remove the top shells from and clean 2 dozen steamed or boiled crabs. Split the crabs in half. Arrange top side up in a broiler pan. Sprinkle garlic powder and lemon pepper generously over crab halves.

Garlic Butter Sauce:

2 sticks butter
3 heaping tablespoons fresh minced garlic
Juice of 1 lemon
¼ bunch parsley, minced

Preheat oven to 350°.

Simmer sauce ingredients together 10 minutes. Add parsley the last 2 minutes. Pour the garlic butter sauce over the crabs. Cover the pan with foil.

Bake for 12 minutes. Eat and enjoy this esteemed Low Country delicacy. Makes 2 dozen garlic crabs.

Chafing-dish Crab with Orange Rice

MARSHA DEAN PHELTS

1 pound Alaskan king crab, frozen or canned
1½ cups sour cream
½ cup sauterne wine
1 teaspoon dried thyme
1 teaspoon salt

Drain the crabmeat and cut into bite-size pieces. Heat the sour cream, sauterne, thyme, and salt in a chafing dish over boiling water or in a double boiler. Add the crabmeat and heat through. Serve over Orange Rice. Serves 6.

Orange Rice:

1 cup orange juice
1 cup chicken bouillon or chicken broth
1 teaspoon salt
1 teaspoon butter or margarine
2 tablespoons minced green onion
1 cup rice

Combine orange juice, bouillon or broth, salt, butter or margarine, and green onion in a saucepan. Bring to a boil and stir in rice. Reduce heat to low and cover saucepan tightly. Steam rice 20 to 25 minutes, or until tender. Serves 6.

Cracked Conch

MARSHA DEAN PHELTS

2 pounds conch steaks
2 cups milk
2 eggs
2 tablespoons water
Juice of 1 lime
Salt and pepper
2 cups self-rising flour
Oil for frying

Have the conch tenderized at the fish market or place of purchase. (To tenderize conch, butchers run whole conchs 2 or 3 times through the same type of machine that cube steaks are put through.) Soak tenderized conch in milk for an hour.

Beat the eggs and water together. Season the soaked conch with lime juice, and salt and pepper to taste. Dredge the conch in flour and shake off excess; dip each side in the beaten egg and water mixture; dredge in flour again. Shake off excess flour and pan-fry both sides in 1 inch hot but not smoking oil to a golden brown. Serve with tartar or cocktail sauce. Serves 4–6.

Crisp Fried Oysters

MARSHA DEAN PHELTS

36 double salted crackers
½ teaspoon salt
¼ teaspoon paprika
¼ teaspoon dried dill weed
2 eggs
2 tablespoons water
1 pint frying oysters, well drained
Fat or oil for frying

With a rolling pin, crush crackers into medium-fine crumbs between two pieces of wax paper; there should be about 2 cups. Mix crumbs well with salt, paprika, and dill weed and divide between two flat plates.

Beat eggs well with water. Dip each oyster on both sides into the first plate of crumbs, then into egg mixture, and finally into the second plate of crumbs. Refrigerate at least 30 minutes to set crumbs. If desired, oysters can be prepared early in the day and refrigerated until needed.

Fry the oysters in moderately hot fat, 365°, until crusty and golden. Do not overcook. Drain on paper towels on a warm platter. Serve with tartar sauce. Serves 3-4.

Occasions to stir up creative menus come frequently in coastal communities. We accept cooking challenges and eat most anything edible from the land and the sea. Seafood is abundant, and it costs next to nothing to figure out an imaginative way to make use of the supply. This squid recipe is a creation that I've enjoyed for many years.

Fried Squid

MARSHA DEAN PHELTS

3 pounds squid
Salt and pepper
Juice of 2 limes

Clean squid by pulling inside entrails and transparent quill (all in one operation). This leaves the squid's inside hollow. Rinse the squid inside and out. Pound each squid gently with the smooth side of a wooden mallet so as not to break the meat. Carefully, by hand, peel the skin from the squid. Salt and pepper the squid to taste and squeeze the lime juice over it. Refrigerate until you are ready to stuff it.

Stuffing:

⅛ cup olive oil
2 tablespoons minced celery
2 tablespoons minced green bell pepper
1 tablespoons minced onions
1 egg
2 cups croutons
1 4-ounce can minced clams
¼ cup chopped walnuts or any chopped nuts

Heat the olive oil until hot but not smoking. Sauté the vegetables until transparent but not brown. In a bowl, beat the egg. Stir in the croutons and combine with the sautéed vegetables. Add the remaining ingredients and mix well. Pack stuffing into the hollowed-out body cavity of each squid, to approximately ¾ inch from the top. Tuck the top inside, over the stuffing.

Batter:

2 eggs, well-beaten
2 cups self-rising flour, sifted
1 cup water or milk

Beat eggs slightly. Gradually beat the flour into the beaten eggs and water or milk to form a batter. Coat the stuffed squid in batter and fry in hot deep fat until golden brown. Remove from the pan and serve hot with your favorite cocktail sauce. Serves 6–8.

11

Too Much Shrimp

Smothered Shrimp
Ernie Albert's Crustacean Delicacy
Coconut Fried Shrimp
Crab–coated Shrimp Chops
Shrimp with Feta
Easter Surprise
Scampi Ron
Shrimp Salsa and Brown Rice
Shrimp Purlo
Shrimp and Sausage Fettuccine
Shrimp Delores with Sauce
Seafood and Vegetable Batter

Never eat more than you can lift.
MISS PIGGY

There are times when residents of American Beach feel that they have had too many shrimp. Other times there may be too many crabs or too much fish. When it comes to too much of an item, people often become more creative and resort to different ways of cooking the same old thing. You can tell when shrimp are plentiful. House pets are fed shrimp omelets, rose gardens flourish due to rich fertilizing with raw shrimp heads. Another sign is that dinner guests are treated to generous servings of shrimp entrées.

Charles Albert, three-time mayor of Fernandina Beach, often reminisces about what he refers to as an impoverished childhood growing up and living on the Amelia River in the sparsely populated Nassauville on the west bank of the Amelia River facing Amelia Island.

After neighborhood fishermen sold their catches at the canneries on the wharf or the fish markets throughout the island, they headed home. The rumbling sounds made by the aged trucks could be heard from a distance as they made their way over the ruts. When these Nassauville fishermen pulled up to a house, the dogs barked and folks ran out front to receive their neighborly offerings. At each homestead, a wooden barrel or old claw-footed porcelain bathtub served as a permanent receptacle for the giveaway catch.

Ernie and Charles Albert, Amelia Island and Nassauville natives.

Seldom did the Albert family enjoy beef or pork, for these meats either had to be bought at the market or slaughtered in season. The bountiful harvest from the sea came in every season; thus islanders frequently availed themselves of the ready supply of food from the sea. The Albert children's having to bring a fish or shrimp sandwich to school for lunch was most embarrassing. However, the fish, the shrimp, the crabs, or the oysters and other foods yielded by the sea or the river were staples in their diet. As children, the young Alberts had no yearning for what they considered poor folks' lunches.

Charles Albert remembers having too many shrimp to cull, clean, and cook. When the Alberts tired of fried shrimp, boiled shrimp, and shrimp Creole, their mother smothered or stewed the shrimp as a last resort.

When selecting shrimp, consider how you will be using them. If you are going to cut shrimp in pieces, medium rather than jumbo is the better size. Shrimp are sold by the pound with reference to the count. Prawns run six to the pound; colossal range from eight to twelve; jumbo, twelve to twenty; large, twenty to thirty; medium, thirty to forty; and small shrimp are more than forty to the pound.

Smothered Shrimp

ERNIE AND CHARLES ALBERT

Juice of 1 lemon
1 pound medium shrimp, peeled and deveined
½ cup Oil
1 large onion, minced
1 green bell pepper, minced
1 egg
2 tablespoons water
½ cup all-purpose flour
1 garlic clove, peeled and minced
2 cups water
1 cup milk or cream
1 teaspoon Worcestershire sauce
1 teaspoon bottled hot pepper sauce
Salt and pepper
2 cups of cooked white rice

Squeeze the lemon juice over the shrimp. In a Dutch oven or deep iron frying pan, heat the oil until hot but not smoking. Sauté the onion and bell pepper until soft, approximately 10 minutes. Set aside.

Beat the egg with the water and coat each shrimp with beaten egg, then flour. Reserve the flour.

Deep-fry the shrimp in a Dutch oven until golden brown. Remove the shrimp and drain on paper towels. Pour the oil from the pot, leaving enough to barely cover the bottom. Add the remaining flour to the oil in the Dutch oven and cook over medium heat, stirring to brown. When the flour has browned, add garlic, bell peppers, and onions. Slowly pour in 2 cups water and 1 cup milk or cream, increasing the heat until the gravy begins to bubble. The amount of water or milk depends on the consistency you want for your gravy. Add Worcestershire sauce, pepper sauce, and salt and pepper to taste. Lower the heat and stir in the shrimp. Let simmer for 20 minutes. Serve with white rice. Serves 4–6.

Ernie Albert's Crustacean Delicacy

3 tablespoons extra-virgin olive oil
1 cup minced onion
1 cup minced green bell pepper
1 cup minced celery
2 beef bouillon cubes
2¼ cups water, divided
2 pounds medium shrimp, peeled and deveined
1 package dry onion soup mix
1 heaping tablespoon all-purpose flour
2 scallions, minced
1 teaspoon soy sauce
Pepper
Cooked rice or grits

Pour the olive oil into an iron frying pan or Dutch oven. Add onions, bell peppers, and celery to the pan and begin to sauté over low heat. Watch carefully, stirring occasionally, as you prepare the rest of the recipe.

Heat ¼ cup water and place the beef bouillon cubes in the water to dissolve. Place the shrimp in a bowl and sprinkle with the onion soup mix and a heaping tablespoon of flour. When the vegetables have softened slightly, stir the shrimp and the scallions into the mixture. Pour the beef bouillon over the shrimp.

Swish 1 cup of water around in the bowl the shrimp were in to release the spicy flavors that remain in bowl. Empty the water into a pan on the stove, add the soy sauce and a few dashes of pepper, and stir. Add the final cup of water and the shrimp mixture to the pan. Cover and simmer a few minutes, until shrimp turn pink. Serve this savory dish over hot rice or grits. Serves 8–10.

$\sim$

A flavorful, fancy, fattening island way of preparing shrimp is to add coconut.

Coconut Fried Shrimp

MARSHA DEAN PHELTS

2 cups all-purpose flour, divided
1½ cups milk
1½ teaspoons baking powder
1 teaspoon curry powder
½ teaspoon salt
2 cups shredded coconut
2 pounds large shrimp, peeled, deveined, tails intact
Oil

In a 1-quart mixing bowl combine 1½ cups flour, the milk, baking powder, curry powder, and salt to make a batter. Place the remaining ½ cup flour and the coconut in separate shallow pans.

Dredge the shrimp in flour, dip in batter, and then roll in coconut. Fry in hot oil at 350° until coconut is golden brown. Drain on paper towels before transferring to a warming tray. Serves 4–6.

Crab-coated Shrimp Chops

MARSHA DEAN PHELTS

1 pound large shrimp, peeled, deveined, butterflied, tails intact
Salt
Juice of 1 lemon, divided
1 pound claw crabmeat
1 tablespoon Worcestershire sauce

1.24-ounce package Old Bay® Crab Cake Classic Seasoning
½ cup mayonnaise, approximately
1 cup all-purpose flour or seafood batter mix

Sprinkle a little salt over the cleaned shrimp, then squeeze the juice of a half lemon over and refrigerate while preparing crab coating mixture.

Place the claw crabmeat in a mixing bowl. Squeeze the rest of the lemon juice and the Worcestershire sauce over the claw meat. Sprinkle seasoning mix over the crabmeat, then add mayonnaise and stir carefully.

Encase each shrimp in the crabmeat mixture, using no more than 2 tablespoons for each. Do not cover the tail. Place shrimp in a single layer in an airtight container and refrigerate at least 4 hours, preferably over-night, to set the coating.

When ready to cook, coat each shrimp chop in flour or seafood mix. Heat oil to 350° and fry the chops until golden. Serves 6–8.

This recipe is straight from *Saveur Magazine*. If you like shrimp, it will become a prized dish.

Shrimp with Feta

SAVEUR MAGAZINE

½ cup extra-virgin olive oil
4 scallions, minced
1 green bell pepper, seeded and
    finely chopped
1 small fresh red chile, seeded and
    finely chopped
1 tablespoon minced fresh oregano
½ cup minced parsley
Freshly ground black pepper
1½ pounds medium shrimp
4 plum tomatoes, peeled, seeded,
    and diced
½ pound feta, crumbled
3 tablespoons milk
Cooked white rice

Heat the oil in a large skillet over medium heat until hot but not smoking. Add the scallions and cook, stirring, until translucent, about 5 minutes.

Add the bell pepper, chiles, oregano, and parsley. Season with pepper to taste and cook, stirring, until bell pepper is soft, about 5 minutes more. Reduce the heat to medium-low. Add the shrimp and cook, stirring occasionally, for 30 minutes. Stir in the tomatoes and cook until they release their juices, about 5 minutes, then add the feta and milk and cook 20 minutes more. Serve over warm rice. Serves 4.

Easter Surprise

MARSHA DEAN PHELTS

8 deviled eggs (see chapter 3 for 2 recipes)
1 pound large shrimp, cooked, peeled and deveined
4 tablespoons butter
4 tablespoons all-purpose flour
¼ teaspoon salt
2 cups canned cream
1 cup shredded sharp cheddar cheese
Cayenne pepper
2 cups crushed potato chips

Preheat oven to 350°.

In a buttered 2½-quart casserole, or 8 individual casserole or seashell dishes, place the deviled eggs and arrange the shrimp around.

Melt the butter in a heavy-bottomed pan; blend in the flour and salt. Stir constantly over low heat for 3 to 4 minutes, until well blended and the taste of raw flour has vanished. Add the cream, continuing to stir, and cook until mixture thickens. Add cheese and cayenne to taste and cook until cheese melts. Pour over eggs and shrimp. Sprinkle the top with crushed potato chips. Bake for 30 minutes. Serves 8.

Scampi Ron

RON KURTZ

2 pounds large shrimp
1 stick butter, divided
5 cloves garlic, peeled and finely minced
⅓ cup olive oil
½ cup dry white wine
Juice of 1 lemon, divided

Salt and pepper
½ cup parsley, including stems, minced, divided
2 cups Basmati rice
1 10-ounce package frozen English peas
Sliced lemons for garnish

Shrimp Preparation:

Remove shells and devein shrimp, leaving tails intact. Rinse well and pat dry, then arrange them in a nonreactive pan suitable for broiling. They will curl as you cook them, so give them room and have them all facing the same way. This makes it easier when placing them on plates. If you are preparing the shrimp early in the day, cover with plastic wrap and refrigerate.

The Sauce:

Melt 2 tablespoons butter in a saucepan and sauté the garlic about 2 minutes. Add the remaining butter and the olive oil, stir, and bring to a light boil. Add the wine and stir, allowing the alcohol to boil off (about 4 minutes). Boil several more minutes, until it smells good enough to eat.

Assembly:

Turn your broiler to high with the door slightly ajar and the top shelf 3 to 5 inches from the broiler unit. Sprinkle the shrimp with half the

Historian Ron Kurtz in the doorway of the Palace Saloon.

juice. Lightly salt and pepper (I am a bit bold with the pepper when using freshly ground). Pour on the sauce and sprinkle half the parsley evenly over the top. Place pan(s) under the broiler for 5 to 7 minutes, until the shrimp are pink. Remove from oven.

The Rice and Peas:

Prepare the basmati rice (which really does smell like popcorn) and the peas according to package directions.

The Presentation:

Divide shrimp evenly for the 8 plates. Lay shrimp along the edge of half of each plate with all tails facing the same direction. Place a slice or two of lemon on each plate. Place a generous helping of rice in the center, making a large well in the middle. Fill the rice well with peas. Sprinkle both rice and shrimp with the remaining parsley and ladle sauce on both. Serves 8.

Shrimp Salsa and Brown Rice

DEBRA MORRISON

2 cups uncooked brown rice
4 cups water
10 ounces frozen corn, thawed
6 scallions, minced
1 red bell pepper, minced
1 green bell pepper, minced
1 16-ounce jar thick and chunky salsa (medium-hot)
⅓ cup olive oil
1 tablespoon fresh lime juice (get a few extra limes for garnish)
1½ teaspoons ground cumin
1 teaspoon grated lime peel
1 pound large shrimp, peeled and cooked (may use fresh or frozen)
Lime wedges
Lime-flavored tortilla chips
Black bean chips

Cook the rice according to package directions, but use less water so the rice is drier. Spoon the hot rice into a bowl and stir in the corn. Refriger-

Debra and Greg Morrison are among the newest American Beach residents.

ate until the mixture is cold, 30 to 40 minutes (it won't spoil the recipe if you leave it in longer). Stir in the scallions and bell peppers.

Blend the salsa, olive oil, lime juice, cumin, and lime peel in a food processor until smooth. Stir half of the sauce into the rice mixture, then add the shrimp and remaining salsa sauce. Mix well. Garnish with lime wedges.

Serve with lime-flavored tortilla chips or black bean chips. The black bean chips are delicious and will add terrific color to your presentation. This is a beautiful and delicious dish. Serves 6.

The Rev. William Holmes's paternal grandmother, "Miss Lizzie" Simmons, who died in 1961 at the age of ninety-two, taught him how to make this dish.

Shrimp Purlo

THE REV. WILLIAM HOLMES

1 cup white rice
8 slices bacon or salt pork, ¼ inch thick
1 large onion, minced

1 medium green bell pepper, minced
2 or 3 cloves garlic, peeled and minced
2½ cups shrimp stock or chicken broth (see chapter 2 for shrimp stock recipe)
Salt and crushed red pepper
1 pound medium shrimp, peeled and deveined

Wash the rice two or three times in a colander and leave to drain.

Cut the bacon or salt pork into 1-inch pieces and cook until crisp in a Dutch oven or suitably sized heavy stockpot. In the same pan cook the onions, bell pepper, and garlic until browned. Add the stock or broth to the pan along with the salt and red pepper to taste and bring to a boil. Add the rice and shrimp but do not stir. Cover and cook on low approximately 30 minutes, or until the liquid has been absorbed and the purlo is dry. Serves 6.

Shrimp and Sausage Fettuccine

KATHIE JEFFERSON CARSWELL

1 pound smoked Kielbasa or other smoked sausage, sliced
½ cup diced onions
½ cup water
½ pound medium shrimp, peeled and deveined
1 tablespoon garlic powder
3 tablespoons butter
1 pound dry fettuccine
1 16-ounce jar Alfredo sauce

Sauté the smoked sausage and onions in a skillet five to ten minutes. Add the water to the pan and cook until onions are translucent. Remove from heat, drain grease from pan, and set aside.

Prepare fettuccine as directed on package. Drain.

Sauté the shrimp in the butter in another pan until pink. Add the sausage mixture to the shrimp and simmer on low for about 5 minutes.

Add the cooked fettuccine to the sausage and shrimp. Stir in Alfredo sauce. Serves 4.

Community activist Kathie Jefferson Carswell is a descendant one of the original Franklin Town families.

Shrimp Delores

MARSHA DEAN PHELTS

Stuffing:

½ loaf stale white bread
2 tablespoons oil
1 large onion, minced
4 ribs celery, minced
4 small garlic cloves, peeled and crushed
1 pound crabmeat
Salt and pepper
1 tablespoon minced pimento
1 egg, beaten
2 tablespoons Worcestershire sauce
2 tablespoons poultry seasoning

Soak the bread in a small amount of water. Heat the oil until hot but not smoking. Sauté the onion, celery, and garlic over low heat until slightly browned. Squeeze most of the water from the bread break into small pieces and add to the onion mixture. Add the crabmeat, stirring over low heat. Add salt and pepper to taste. Add the minced pimento. Pour the egg over the mixture and stir until well blended. Add the Worcestershire sauce and poultry seasoning, stir well, and remove from heat.

Shrimp:

30 large shrimp, tail intact
2 tablespoons butter, melted
2 tablespoons water

Preheat oven to 375°.

Slit shrimp down the center of the back and remove the vein. Put the butter and water in a 13-inch × 18-inch baking sheet and carefully place rounded portions of stuffing in the slit of each shrimp. Place shrimp, stuffed side up, close together on the baking sheet. Bake 15 minutes.

Sauce:

1 stick butter or margarine
3 tablespoons Worcestershire sauce
⅓ cup cooking sherry
Juice of ½ lemon

While shrimp are baking, mix all sauce ingredients in a saucepan and simmer over low heat for about 8 minutes. Pour over baked, stuffed shrimp and serve hot. Serves 6.

∾

During my childhood in the 1950s, Morrison's restaurants were a forbidden experience for people of color. They had a reputation second to none for fine food. Oh, the food from this restaurant chain was well known! Anyone within hollering distance knew how good this place must be, because the lines at lunch and dinner came out the door and wrapped around the building every day. This restaurant employed the best cooks, servers, and waiters to be found, and they were all black people.

The opportunity to experience the cuisine of this establishment came to us with the passage in 1964 of the Civil Rights Act. A popular dish throughout the restaurant's years of operation was its fried shrimp. Here is Morrison's recipe for the batter used on seafood and vegetables such as fried green tomatoes, eggplant, okra, squash, mushrooms, and onions.

Seafood and Vegetable Batter

4¼ cups all-purpose flour, divided
2 tablespoons baking powder
1¼ teaspoons salt
3 teaspoons paprika
1 egg, lightly beaten
3 cups cold water
1 teaspoon garlic salt
Seafood or vegetables of your choice

Sift together 3¼ cups flour, the baking powder, salt and paprika. Whisk in the beaten egg, water, and garlic salt and blend well.

Season seafood (such as shrimp, cleaned but with tails attached) or vegetables with salt and pepper. Dredge in the remaining flour and then dip in the batter. Fry in vegetable oil heated to 350° until golden brown.

Note: This makes enough batter for 3 pounds of shrimp; you may want to halve the recipe.

12

Seafood Galore

Seafood Creole
Shrimp Creole
Crab–Shrimp Bake
Sweet–Sour Shrimp and Apple Stir–fry with Sauce
Fran's Paella
Soul Man's Crab Boil
Fruit of the Sea

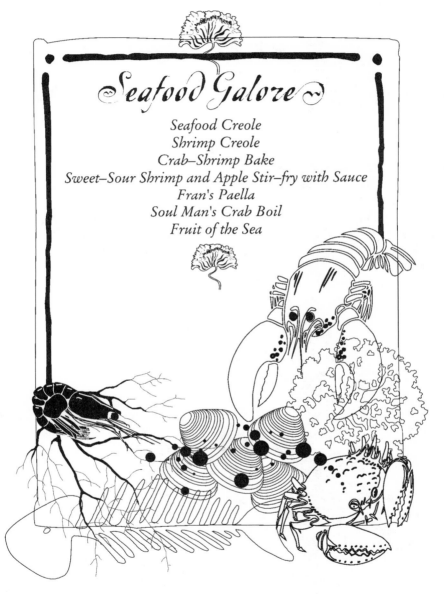

When I am old and gray, I want to have a house by the sea. . . . With a lot of wonderful chums, good music and booze around. And a damn good kitchen to cook in.

AVA GARDNER

Annette McCollough Myers, former president of the American Beach Property Owners Association, has been the owner of the historic Miss Martha's Hideaway on American Beach since 1960.

Annette was born on Amelia Island and comes from a seafaring family, community, and town. She states that seafood was their livelihood. Her father, Wendell McCollough, owned his shrimp boat. Annette united with another seafaring family when she married Elmo Myers of nearby St. Mary's, Georgia. Elmo was the captain of his own ship and sailed far and near following shrimp.

Early on, Annette experienced the preparation and eating of a wide variety of seafood. She has cooked a varied range of seafood and enjoys the delicate taste of squid. When it comes to eel, she draws the line. She's had many opportunities to try her hand at eating or preparing eel but never had a desire to work with this snakelike fish.

When asked for her favorite recipe, Annette fondly remembered this one she created for her husband's shrimp boat crew. Though she hasn't prepared this recipe in years, she recalls that it was a hit with locals and

Annette McCollough Myers's roots run deep through the island. Here she is celebrating the publication of her book, *The Shrinking Sands of an African American Beach*.

that they served it during the cold wintry months or in drumfish season.

Annette describes drumfish season as when gnats are biting. Gnats are a nuisance during the summer months, and that's when large drumfish bite as well. Nowadays, Annette favors serving a seafood creole using shrimp with a combination of fish, crabs, scallops, squid, or whatever else the catch of the day is.

Seafood Creole

ANNETTE MCCOLLOUGH MYERS

2 tablespoons oil
1 green bell pepper, minced
½ cup minced onion
½ cup diced celery
1 tablespoon minced garlic
1 6-ounce can tomato paste
1½ cups water
1 teaspoon salt

1 bay leaf
1 teaspoon thyme
⅛ teaspoon black pepper
⅛ teaspoon monosodium glutamate, optional
2 cups cooked seafood
Cooked rice

Heat the oil in a saucepan until hot but not smoking. Sauté the bell pepper, onion, celery, and garlic until tender. Add tomato paste, water, and seasonings. Simmer 15 minutes, stirring occasionally. Add seafood and heat through. Serve over hot seasoned brown rice or other rice of your choice. Serves 6.

Shrimp Creole

LOIS ISZARD

¼ cup margarine or butter
1 large onion, minced
1 medium green pepper, sliced
1 clove garlic, minced
½ teaspoon salt
Pepper

⅛ teaspoon paprika
3½ cups fresh or canned tomatoes
1 pound medium shrimp, cleaned and cooked
3 cups hot cooked rice

Melt the butter or margarine in a saucepan. Add the onion, green pepper, and garlic and sauté 10 minutes, or until tender. Add the salt, a dash of pepper, paprika, and tomatoes and bring to a boil. Reduce the heat and simmer 15 minutes. Add the shrimp and heat thoroughly. Serve over hot rice. Serves 6.

Crab-Shrimp Bake

LOIS ISZARD

1 medium green bell pepper, minced
1 medium onion, minced
1 cup minced celery
1 6½- or 7½-ounce can crabmeat, flaked
1 cup medium shrimp, cleaned and cooked
½ teaspoon salt
Pepper
1 teaspoon Worcestershire sauce
1 cup mayonnaise
1 cup buttered dried bread crumbs

Preheat oven to 350°.

Combine all ingredients but crumbs and place in individual seashells or a greased 3-quart casserole. Sprinkle with buttered crumbs and bake about 30 minutes. Serves 6.

Bud Coe, an Amelia Island architect and historic preservationist, drew the plans for the home that would replace the most recognized landmark home on American Beach, the Blue Palace. A multitalented individual, Bud has cultivated his culinary skills to a fine and tasteful art. He has created over 100 recipes for shrimp. This is a most delicate treatment of crustaceans with fruit flavors and delicate summer vegetables.

Sweet-Sour Shrimp and Apple Stir-Fry

BUD COE

3 tablespoons oil, divided
1 pound shrimp, peeled and deveined
2 golden delicious apples, cored and thinly sliced
1 cup green onion, cut into 1-inch lengths
1 medium green bell pepper, cut into strips
8 ounces snow peas

½ cup plus 2 tablespoons water
⅓ cup firmly packed light brown sugar
¼ cup white vinegar
1 teaspoon soy sauce
1 teaspoon ground ginger
4 teaspoons cornstarch
Cooked rice or chow mein noodles

Heat 1 tablespoon oil over high heat and sauté shrimp until pink. Remove the shrimp from the pan. Add 1 tablespoon oil to the pan and sauté the apple slices for 1 minute. Remove the apple slices from the pan. Add the remaining tablespoon of oil, the green onions, bell pepper, and snow peas. Sauté 2 minutes and remove from the pan. Combine ½ cup water, brown sugar, vinegar, soy sauce, and ginger in a pan large enough to hold

The Blue Palace was left in ruins from Hurricane Dora, September 9, 1964.

The Dawkins home, designed by Bud Coe, historic preservation architect, occupies the site where the Blue Palace once stood.

all the ingredients and bring to a boil. Dissolve the cornstarch in 2 table-spoons water and add to soy mixture. Cook until thickened. Return all ingredients to the pan and heat thoroughly. Serve immediately over rice or chow mein noodles. Serves 4–6.

Sweet and Sour Sauce:

½ cup catsup
⅓ cup orange marmalade
3 tablespoons red wine vinegar
1 tablespoon soy sauce

1 tablespoon lemon juice
2 teaspoons dry mustard
1 teaspoon prepared horseradish
¼ teaspoon curry powder

Mix all ingredients in a saucepan and heat until hot and bubbly. Serve warm. Approximately 1 cup.

The Jollivettes have been property owners on the beach founded by Mary McLeod Bethune for over half a century. When Dr. Jollivette was alive, the family spent annual vacations on American Beach. This is Russ Jollivette's favorite recipe of his mother's.

Fran's Paella

FRANCES JOLLIVETTE-CHAMBERS

The Meat:

6 ounces chicken wings
6 ounces pork, cubed
1 tablespoon olive oil
1 tablespoon white vinegar
½ teaspoon minced fresh rosemary
½ teaspoon minced fresh thyme
Salt and pepper

Put the chicken and pork in a bowl and add olive oil, vinegar, herbs, and salt and pepper to taste. Stir to coat.

The Paella:

⅓ cup olive oil
½ cup green bell pepper, cut in ½-inch cubes
½ cup red bell pepper, cut in ½-inch cubes

4 tablespoons minced parsley
4 garlic cloves, peeled and minced
4 cups long-grain white rice
6 large cracked stone crab claws
6 clams
6 mussels
6 large prawns
2 cups boiling chicken broth

1 18-ounce can tomato sauce
1 cup beer
1 16-ounce can early peas, drained
1 fresh rosemary sprig
1 teaspoon crushed red pepper
¼ teaspoon saffron
¼–½ teaspoon sweet paprika

For the paella, heat the olive oil at very high heat until hot but not smoking and sauté the pork and chicken pieces until golden in color and glazed on all sides. Use a 4-quart Dutch oven. Add the bell peppers and sauté about 2 minutes, stirring constantly. Add the parsley and stir to mix well. Push the ingredients to the sides of the pan and add the garlic to the center. Garlic is given a clean place in the pan so that the cooking can be monitored separately from the seasonings pushed to the side, as garlic doesn't require as much cooking. Mix the ingredients well. Add the rice and stir to coat well with oil, about 1 minute. Add the seafood and stir to mix well. Stir in the tomato sauce, boiling chicken broth, beer, peas, and rosemary sprig, red pepper, and saffron, and spread the ingredients evenly around the pan. Cook until the broth is reduced enough for the rice to begin showing. Do not stir. Lower the heat and simmer uncovered for 10 to 12 minutes. The paella should look dry and the top layer of rice fairly firm. Remove from heat, sprinkle top with paprika, and cover loosely with a paper towel, and allow to rest 10 minutes before serving. Serves 6.

Soul Man's Crab Boil

BONNIE AND WILLIE C. SCOTT

3 pounds neck bones
3 pounds pigs' feet, split
Salt and crushed red pepper
3 quarts water
1 quart beer
4 large onions, quartered

1 rib celery, cut in large pieces
1 peeled garlic bulb
2 large green bell peppers
3 pounds red potatoes, with skins
1 box crab boil
3 dozen live blue crabs

In a 5-gallon heavy stockpot (a government pot), place neck bones and pigs' feet that have been seasoned with salt and crushed red pepper to taste. Add the water and beer, bring to a boil, cover pot, and simmer 2 hours, or until meats are tender.

Add the onions, celery, garlic bulb, bell peppers, and potatoes (potatoes may be left whole or halved, depending on their size), and crab boil. Continue cooking for 10 minutes, or until potatoes are tender but not mushy. Return the pot to a high rolling boil and toss in the live blue crabs. Add any other spices you choose and cook for 20. Serves 12.

Girls' night out in 1965 at the American Beach shoreline. From left, Bonnie Matthews Scott, her sister Bernice Graham Brown, Shirley Ann Jackson, and Helen Brown.

Fruit of the Sea

LISA VANDER WEGE

1 pound jumbo shrimp, steamed, peeled, and deveined
½ pound sugar snap peas, blanched
1 pint grape tomatoes
1 yellow bell pepper, julienned
1 pound rice noodles, prepared according to package directions
½ cup olive oil
½ cup fresh lemon juice
2 cloves garlic, peeled and minced
½ cup minced parsley
Fresh cracked pepper
1 pound sea scallops
1 pound squid tubes, sliced in rings
Sea salt
Pepper

Toss together all of the ingredients but the scallops and squid, salt and pepper to taste. Heat a 12-inch skillet to medium-high and quickly sear the scallops and squid, being careful not to overcook. Add to the salad and then add salt and pepper to taste. Serves 10–12.

Jamie Vendola, Audrey Lott, Lisa Vander Wege, Jenny Terpening, and Stephanie Christopher. Lisa Vander Wege is the owner of Gourmet Gourmet Restaurant on American Beach. The restaurant is rated among the top on the First Coast.

13

Fish, Fish in a Dish

Fried Drum Ribs
Baked Fish
Red Snapper with Smashin' Salsa
Pompano en Papillotte
Red and White Blue Fish
Smothered Catfish Nuggets

There are over 600 species of fish found in the fresh and salt waters of Florida.
Florida fishing is still the best in the nation.

T. N. ANDERSON

Poignant memories surface as I reflect on the spring Sunday morning that we ate cheese grits topped with Grannie's tomato gravy and crisp fried ribs hacked from the backbone of an enormous drumfish. The day before, my neighbor Charles Kirtsey, a retiree from Rayonier Paper Mill, had caught and butchered a sixty-pound drum. After chopping up fish steaks, he shared the ribs with neighbors. He was accustomed to dividing big catches. Back when he was growing up on the island, fish and game were routinely apportioned to family and friends, as there was no means of keeping them fresh for a long period of time.

He grew up eating drum once a year in a fish stew or bouillabaisse, with all sorts of garden vegetables and stimulating spices. To clean this man-sized fish, the scales were raked from the body with a garden hoe. The head of the drumfish served as the main ingredient for a stew; other parts are prepared several ways. People stewed, boiled, barbecued, or fried the drums caught and shared until no flesh of the fish remained.

I had never seen ribs cut from the backbone. At the fish market on the dock, the meat was cut away from the fish and the entire carcass, including the head, was tossed back into the inlet for sea turtles and pelicans to feast on. The rib bones from the fish Kirtsey gave me were about seven to twelve inches long. We ate them by holding the end of the bone between our fingertips and the meat simply slipped from the bone with a slight tug of our teeth. So easy, like removing the peel from a banana. I thought that I had ascended to paradise with my eyes wide open. The next morning, I carried a bag of bleach-washed fish ribs to school for my own show and tell. I placed the bones on each table in my library for examination and observation. The students and teachers were as excited as I was about them.

Fried Drum Ribs

CHARLES KIRTSEY

2 pounds drum ribs or fillets
Sea salt and pepper
Juice of 1 lemon
2 tablespoons bottled hot pepper sauce
1 cup cornmeal
Oil

Season ribs with salt and pepper to taste, hot pepper sauce, and lemon juice and allow to marinate for 20 minutes. Heat oil to 350°. Coat ribs with meal and drop in hot oil. Remove from oil when ribs turn golden and rise to the top. Serves 6.

Baked Fish

MIRIAM CUNNINGHAM BURNEY

1 trout or other fish, 2–4 pounds
Salt and pepper
4 slices bacon, halved
2 lemons, thinly sliced
½ large onion, sliced
½ large green bell pepper, sliced
2 tablespoons olive oil
1 28-ounce can tomatoes
1 tablespoon all-purpose flour or cornstarch
⅓ cup cold water

Preheat oven to 350°.

Season the whole fish with a small amount of salt. Make 3 or 4 slits in each side of the fish and alternate bacon and lemon slices in slits. Lightly grease a baking pan with olive oil. Place the fish in the pan and bake for 15 minutes.

While the fish is baking, sauté the onion and bell pepper in the remaining olive oil until soft. Add the tomatoes and simmer for 20 minutes. Mix the flour or cornstarch in ⅓ cup cold water until smooth. Pour the mixture into the pan and continue cooking for 10 minutes. Serves 4–6.

Red Snapper and Smashin' Salsa

DENNIS STEWART (MR. NATURAL)

2 pounds snapper or grouper fillets
Juice of 2 limes
1 teaspoon seasoned salt
1 tablespoon olive oil
1 white onion, sliced in rings
1 green bell pepper, cut in strips
1 cup spicy salsa

Coat the fish with lime juice and sprinkle with seasoned salt. Brush half of the olive oil on the fillets, onion rings, and green pepper strips, and grill or broil until firm to the touch. Later in this recipe you will see that one cup of the Salsa goes over the fish along with the vegetables. While fillets are cooking, sauté onions and bell pepper.

Smashin' Salsa:

1 cup seeded and diced fresh
  tomatoes
½ cup minced green onion
½ tomatillo, diced
1 teaspoon lime juice
1 tablespoon apple cider vinegar
½ small jalapeño pepper

Pinch of salt
1 clove garlic, peeled and minced
Few drops fresh ginger juice
Fresh summer vegetables, sliced
4 tablespoons olive oil
Salt and pepper to taste

Combine all ingredients for salsa and chill at least 1 hour.

Slice summer vegetables in season, such as squash, mushrooms, broccoli, and carrots. Heat olive oil in a 10-inch skillet until hot but not smoking and sauté vegetables and salsa for 5 to 10 minutes. Add a little salt and pepper. Cook just until tender. Serve vegetables and Smashin' Salsa over grilled fish. Serves 4–6.

Dennis Stewart Jr. on American Beach for the Fourth of July (1948).

Every now and then, I run across a nice catch of pompano that an angler has caught from the surf. When these delicacies come my way we are in store for a gourmet dinner.

Pompano en Papillote

NEIL FRINK

3 medium-sized pompano (you may substitute rainbow trout, sea bass, or other pan-sized white meat fish)
3 cups water
1 bay leaf
Salt and freshly ground pepper
6 green onions, minced
6 tablespoons butter or margarine, divided
2 cups dry white wine
2 tablespoons all-purpose flour
1 cup chopped cooked shrimp
1 cup crabmeat
½ clove garlic, peeled and minced
2 egg yolks, beaten
parchment paper

Clean the fish, removing heads and backbones. Cook heads and backbones in 3 cups water with the bay leaf and salt and pepper to taste, place fish in cold water then bring to a boil. Reduce stock to 2 cups.

Preheat oven to 400°.

Melt 4 tablespoons of butter or margarine in a skillet and sauté the onions for 4 minutes. Add the fish and wine, cover, and simmer gently until fillets are tender, about 5 minutes. Remove the fish, open flat, and place each on a sheet of parchment or greased brown paper.

Melt the remaining butter in another saucepan over medium heat. Add the flour and cooked onions and brown slightly. Add fish stock and cook until sauce thickens, about 5 minutes. Stir in the shrimp, crabmeat, and salt to taste. Remove from the heat and stir in the egg yolks. Spoon the sauce over fillets. Fold the paper to form a case around each fillet. Bake for 10 minutes. To serve, split paper and fold back. Serves 3.

Bluefish are good biters and easy to catch on American Beach and along the northeast Atlantic coastline. They are common fish in this community; local fish markets don't carry them because people won't buy them, for there is no need to. Surf fishermen give bluefish away as freely as catfish; they are treated as throwaways or giveaways, whatever comes first. My ample supply of bluefish comes from Ron Miller and his wife, Lynnette, who host fish fries all over the beach.

While locals don't buy bluefish, surf fishermen package their plentiful catch and go to neighboring counties, where they peddle it for a dollar a piece. Of course, these fishermen don't call these fish bluefish because we look down on bluefish just as we do catfish and mullet. But off the ocean they give bluefish a fancy name and inlanders purchase them by the bagful.(Fish hawkers call them Ocean Blue Streamers and people will buy them with that name, rather than buying them as bluefish.) When we travel off the island we get quite a chuckle to see the cost of bluefish on restaurant menus.

A local, Ronnie Dawson, formerly of Baltimore, has high regard for the bluefish. According to one of this fellow's many fish tales, the bluefish that are caught on the northeast Florida Atlantic coast are en route from Florida via Georgia and the Carolinas to offshore Virginia Beach. When the bluefish swim their way to the top of Chesapeake Bay, they take a right turn to the northeast toward Delaware and head back to the ocean and keep swimming north. By the time these fish leave the Tidewater region of Chesapeake Bay, where they feed heavily upon the plentiful food supply, the blues are a whopping twenty pounds.

Big blues like that are not seen around American Beach, but the two-to six-pound blues caught at the American Beach shoreline are plenty big enough to cook and enjoy. Dawson advises that bluefish have sharp teeth and powerful jaws and are vicious. When you catch a blue, cut the hook from your line and remove the head from the fish or kill it immediately in order to prevent the blood from getting into the meat. A fish killed within one hour of being caught has a much better flavor than one that has lingered in a bucket. In his oceanfront flat, Dawson works the foot-long blues into a sensational entrée that would take a seafood connoisseur to ecstasy.

Red and White Blue Fish

RONNIE DAWSON

4 whole foot-long bluefish or 4 8-ounce fillets
4 scallions, minced
½ red bell pepper, minced
2 seeded and minced finger peppers
12 sprigs parsley, minced
4 sprigs fresh oregano, stems discarded, minced
Juice of 1 lemon or lime
4 ounces honey mustard
4-ounce can sliced mushrooms and stems, drained
8 tablespoons fine dry bread crumbs, divided
Paprika
4 teaspoons margarine or butter

Preheat oven to 400°.

After cleaning the fish remove the head and backbone and butterfly the fish. Coat the skin side of each fish with 1 teaspoon butter or margarine and place it skin side down on a sheet of aluminum foil large enough to cover it.

In a bowl mix the scallions, bell pepper, finger peppers, parsley, and oregano. Stir in the lemon or lime juice, honey mustard, and mushrooms. Divide the sauce evenly among the fish, then sprinkle each fish with 2 tablespoons bread crumbs and paprika. Seal the aluminum foil.

Place the foil-covered fish in a baking pan and bake for 10 minutes. Open the foil and cook uncovered for 10 minutes, or until fish flakes easily with a fork. Do not overcook. Serves 4.

In many fishing communities, catfish are unappreciated and looked on as nuisance fish. Catfish have sharp fins that make them dangerous to handle without heavy gloves. Because of their tough skin, they have to be peeled with pliers. Cleaning them is difficult and takes a lot of time; thus it's hard to give them away, so many fishermen throw them away. Crossing the many bridges to the island, you can see the carcasses of catfish that fisherman have cut from their lines and discarded.

Catfish are, however, simply delicious and can be prepared a variety of ways. I never pass up an opportunity to eat fried catfish fingerlings. Six

The Thornton siblings after the state fair in Bronson, Florida (1958). From left, Deloris, Warren, Altamese, Dale, and Brenda.

small catfish usually make a single serving in restaurants. If it takes six to make an order, then this is a good indicator that the catfish are fingerlings and the restaurant knows its business.

In fish markets and supermarkets, catfish fillets and nuggets can be bought inexpensively. When you see them at a bargain price, please follow this easy recipe exactly. You'll never see catfish as trash fish again and you'll thank Deloris Gilyard for this finding.

Smothered Catfish Nuggets

DELORIS GILYARD

3 pounds catfish nuggets
Salt and pepper
1 cup self-rising flour
Oil
2 large onions, minced
2 bell peppers, minced, any color

1 hot pepper, minced
1 tablespoon Worcestershire sauce
2–3 cups water, divided
Steamed white rice

Season fish with salt and pepper to taste, then dredge in flour; shake off excess and reserve the flour. Heat several inches of oil to 350° in a Dutch oven or deep iron frying pan and fry the fish until golden; set nuggets aside. Pour off oil, leaving only enough to sauté the onions and peppers. Let the peppers and onions cook down for 10 minutes, then remove half and set aside. Sprinkle the remaining flour over the vegetables in the pan, add Worcestershire sauce and 1 cup water, and increase the heat. Add another cup of water and stir as mixture begins to bubble. If the gravy is too thick, add a third cup of water. Lower the heat.

Return the fish to the pan of gravy, top with reserved onions and peppers, cover, and simmer for 5 minutes. Serve over a bed of steamed white rice. Serves 8–10.

At home with Erving and Deloris Gilyard for their annual Christmas brunch.

14

Poultry

Late–night Chicken Pot
Momma's Southern–fried Chicken
Chicken and Scampi
Stewed Chicken and Dumplings
Cornbread Dumplings
Aunt Liza's Curried Chicken
Maharani Chicken Curry
Chicken Tetrazzini
Pressed Chicken
Daddy Charlie's Jamaican con Pollo

*I want there to be no peasant in my realm so poor
that he will not have a chicken in his pot every Sunday.*

HENRI IV OF FRANCE

When American Beach observed its seventieth anniversary year on January 31, 2005, the Rev. Dr. Carlton D. Jones was installed as president of the American Beach Property Owners Association. Bursts of activity to commemorate the anniversary were planned for each month in the year. Jones continued building upon foundations laid by previous presidents Annette M. Myers and Judge Henry Lee Adams, Jr. On Presidents' Day, February 19, 2007, Jones was sworn in for his second term as the seventh president of the association and the silver anniversary president, as the association celebrated its twenty-fifth year.

Jones and his wife, Barbara, hail from large families (in Washington, D.C., and Miami, Florida, respectively). They are surrounded by an even larger band of friends. For the Joneses entertaining is business. Their hospitality has favorably spoiled and enriched this community. When historic American Beach has a celebration, "everybody is welcomed."

An architecture planner and builder, Jones moved the American Beach enclave to another level. American Beach is and always has been a community of privately owned property. Jones, a member of the Florida Advisory Council of the Trust for Public Land, has worked to ensure the future

Entertaining is a routine part of business for the family of Barbara and the Reverend Dr. Carlton D. Jones.

of American Beach. Under his leadership and by working with preservation and land trusts, ten acres on and off the oceanfront have now become public lands, preserving American Beach and Evans' Rendezvous.

Late-night Chicken Pot

CARLTON JONES

1 cut up chicken (10 pieces)
Salt and pepper
Oil
2 medium onions cut in ¾-inch pieces
1 large green pepper cut in ¾-inch pieces
4 ribs celery sliced in ¾-inch pieces
2 cups white rice
2 14-ounce cans chicken broth
1 6-ounce can tomato paste
3 medium potatoes, peeled and diced
2 carrots, scraped and sliced
1 16-ounce package frozen English peas, thawed

Season the chicken with salt and pepper to taste. Heat 2 to 3 inches of oil in a heavy Dutch oven until hot but not smoking. Brown the chicken slightly, until the fat is rendered. Add the rice and chicken broth. Stir in the tomato paste and bring to boil. Add the remaining ingredients and return to a boil. Cover and simmer for 40 minutes. Serves 8.

Momma's Southern-fried Chicken

VIRGINIA MCKINNEY MEALING

2 chicken fryers, cut up, or chicken parts, cut up (legs, wings, thighs, breasts)
Salt and pepper
Garlic powder or other seasonings as desired
1 cup all-purpose flour
2 eggs, beaten
½ cup milk
Vegetable shortening or oil

Wash the chicken and pat dry. Place it in a bowl or on wax paper. Heat the shortening or oil in a frying pan until hot but not smoking. (Although vegetable oils are more healthful, the best fried chicken is made with shortening.) The key to frying chicken is making sure the fat is hot and that there is enough oil in the frying pan to cover the chicken pieces.

Mix seasonings and flour. Mix eggs and milk in a wide bowl. Dip each piece of chicken in the egg mixture and then in flour. Shake off excess flour and place the chicken piece in hot oil; do not crowd. Fry on one side until a nice golden brown; turn and brown on the other side. (Optional: Cover the pan with a screen or lid until the first side is cooked. Finish cooking uncovered.)

Remove the chicken from the pan and drain on paper towels. Serves 10.

∾

Chicken and Scampi was a dish that Netty Johnson Leapheart's friends looked forward to eating as they accepted her much-sought-after invitations to visit during annual vacations on the beach. Each year during the 1950s and the 1960s, Netty, office manager of the Jacksonville office of the Atlanta Life Insurance Company, rented the Broadnax home. Summers at

Netty Leapheart (*left*) and Clara Johnson with a mess of fish (1950).

Vacationing on American Beach was an annual ritual for Netty Leapheart's family. Netty (circa 1930s).

the beach were a retreat for the gathering of family and friends. The large entourage swam, fished, shelled, and crabbed from the shore and bridge. Their catches were bountiful, and they celebrated by cooking their daily catches. As hostess and meal planner, Netty put together staples and seasonings to concoct this savory dish of chicken and shrimp.

Chicken and Scampi

NETTY LEAPHEART

3½-pound broiler-fryer, cut up
1 tablespoon salt
½ teaspoon pepper
Oil
3 small onions, minced
1 clove garlic, peeled and minced
3 tablespoons snipped parsley plus more for garnish
½ cup port wine
1 8-ounce can tomato sauce
1 teaspoon dried basil
1 pound medium shrimp, peeled and deveined

Rub the chicken well with salt and pepper. Heat 2 to 3 inches oil in a frying pan until hot but not smoking. Sauté the chicken until golden on all sides. Add the onions, garlic, 3 tablespoons parsley, port, tomato sauce, and basil and simmer, covered, about 30 minutes, or until chicken is tender.

Push the chicken pieces to one side and bring the tomato mixture to a boil. Add the shrimp and cook, uncovered, 3 to 4 minutes, or until shrimp just turns pink.

Pile golden chicken pieces in a serving dish and top with pink shrimp. Skim all fat from the sauce and pour the sauce over the chicken and scampi. Sprinkle on a little snipped parsley. Serves 6.

Stewed Chicken and Dumplings

DENNIS STEWART (MR. NATURAL)

1 hen, 4–6-pounds, cut up
2 quarts water
1 large onion, coarsely chopped
2 ribs celery, coarsely chopped
1 large green bell pepper
2 bay leaves
2 large cloves garlic, thinly sliced
½ teaspoon salt
1 teaspoon freshly ground black pepper

Dumplings:

2 cups all-purpose flour
2½ teaspoons baking powder
½ teaspoon salt
1 egg, beaten
½ cup water

Heat 2 to 3 inches oil in a heavy, large Dutch oven until hot but not smoking. Brown chicken on all sides. Add the water, onion, celery, bell pepper, bay leaves, garlic, and salt and pepper. Bring to a boil and skim off foam. Reduce the heat, cover, and simmer until the chicken is tender, about 2 hours. Let the chicken cool in the broth for about an hour. Remove the chicken from the broth and set aside in a warming pan in oven.

Skim rendered fat from the broth. Simmer the broth uncovered until it has reduced to 1 quart. Meanwhile, make dumplings.

In a large bowl, combine the flour, baking powder, and salt. Cut in the shortening with a pastry blender or fork until the mixture resembles coarse meal. Blend the egg and water and stir into dry ingredients to make a soft dough.

Return the chicken broth to a boil, then return the chicken to the broth. Drop small spoonfuls of dough, a few at a time, into boiling broth. When all the dumplings are in the pot, reduce heat to low and simmer, covered, until the dumplings are done, about 20 minutes. Serves 5.

~

Many times Mama had to improvise on chicken and dumplings. When she ran out of flour she substituted cornmeal, and these dumplings were equally as good.

Dumplings had faded as a staple in American cuisine long before the consumption of carbohydrates became a four-letter word. This recipe for cornbread dumplings is included as a poignant reminder of a dining tradition.

Cornbread Dumplings

EVA R. LAMAR

1½ cups cornmeal
4 tablespoons all-purpose flour, optional
2 teaspoons salt, optional
1 teaspoon sugar
1 cup boiling water
Chicken broth

Combine cornmeal, flour (if using), salt (if using), and sugar. Add boiling water and stir constantly until the mixture forms a stiff dough. Form small balls of dough with a tablespoon and drop them into boiling broth. Cook slowly, covered, for 20 minutes. Makes 15 dumplings.

Aunt Liza's Curried Chicken

ELIZA ROSIER GLASS

1 stick butter or margarine
4 tart apples, minced
4 medium onions, minced

2 garlic cloves, peeled and minced
4 tablespoons all-purpose flour
1 pint chicken broth
2 teaspoons curry powder
Salt and pepper
Worcestershire sauce
Bottled hot pepper sauce
Juice of 1 lemon
1 cup pineapple juice
6 pounds seasoned, cooked, cut-up chicken
Hot cooked white rice
Freshly grated toasted coconut, for garnish
Chutney
Crisp crumbled bacon, for garnish
Grated hard-boiled eggs, for garnish
Minced scallions, for garnish
Minced green bell pepper, for garnish
Seedless raisins or currants, for garnish

Preheat oven to 325°.

Melt the butter or margarine in an ovenproof casserole. Brown the apples, onions, and garlic. Stir in the flour and chicken broth until smooth. Stirring constantly, add the curry powder, salt and pepper to taste, Worcestershire sauce, hot pepper sauce, lemon juice, and pineapple juice. Add the chicken and bake for 30 minutes.

Serve over hot white rice with bowls of fresh grated toasted coconut, chutney, crisp broken bacon pieces, toasted peanuts, grated hard-boiled eggs, minced scallions, minced bell peppers, and seedless raisins or currants. Serves 10.

Maharani Chicken Curry

ALEXANDER HICKSON

2½-pound broiler-fryer, cut up
¼ cup butter or margarine
1½ cups minced onion
½ clove garlic, peeled and minced
1½ teaspoons ground ginger
1 cup diced fresh tomato

1 teaspoon salt
3–4 dashes medium or hot curry powder, or to taste
2-inch cinnamon stick
Seeds from 1 small cardamom pod
1 teaspoon turmeric
1 teaspoon ground cumin
1 teaspoon paprika
1 teaspoon crushed red pepper flakes
⅓ cup plain yogurt
1 cup coconut flakes, fresh or dried
½ cup currants
½ cup yellow raisins

Wash the chicken and dry with paper towels. Remove the skin and discard. Melt the butter or margarine in a large skillet with a tight-fitting lid and sauté the chicken until nicely browned all over—10 to 15 minutes; remove. Add the onion, garlic, and ginger and sauté until golden—about 10 minutes. Add the tomato, salt, curry powder, cinnamon stick, cardamom seeds, turmeric, cumin, paprika, and red pepper flakes; cover and cook over low heat 3 minutes. Stir in the yogurt until well blended. Add the chicken pieces and simmer, covered, turning chicken occasionally, 30

People from all over the island attended gatherings at Alexander Hickson's beach cottage (1990).

to 40 minutes, or until the chicken is fork-tender. Arrange the chicken on a platter and spoon on sauce. Serves 4.

Maharani chicken curry is Alexander's signature recipe. He suggests serving this Indian dish over Uncle Ben's rice and topping the dish with sprinkles of coconut, currants, and yellow raisins. To complete this meal you need only a good mixed green salad and a glass of chilled Chardonnay.

Chicken Tetrazzini

BEVERLY MCKENZIE

4 tablespoons butter or margarine
4 cups diced cooked chicken
1 8-ounce box spaghetti, broken into 1-inch pieces and cooked according to package directions
2 cups heavy cream sauce
1 cup chicken broth
1 4-ounce can sliced mushrooms, drained
4 ounces pimentos, minced
8 ounces New York cheddar, cubed
¼ cup Parmesan cheese
½ cup buttered fresh or dried bread crumbs

Preheat oven to 325°.

In a large saucepan melt the butter or margarine. Pour off 1 tablespoon into a 9-inch × 13-inch glass casserole dish to coat bottom and sides. Reserve 2 tablespoons for later use. Add the chicken, cooked spaghetti, cream sauce, chicken broth, mushrooms, pimentos, and cheddar cheese to the saucepan and blend well. Pour into the greased casserole dish. Sprinkle evenly with Parmesan cheese and buttered bread crumbs. Bake 40 minutes, or until hot and breadcrumbs are nicely browned. Serves 8.

Pressed Chicken

MARSHA DEAN PHELTS

4 tablespoons plain gelatin
½ cup plus 2½ tablespoons cold water
2 cups boiling chicken broth

4 cups diced cooked and seasoned chicken
2½ teaspoons lemon juice
8 tablespoons mayonnaise
6 hard-boiled eggs, peeled and sieved
3 cups minced celery
Buttered nuts, as garnish

Soak the gelatin in 2½ tablespoons cold water. This is correct. After it has dissolved completely, pour the boiling broth over it. Cool. When the gelatin is cool, add all other ingredients and pour the mix into a cold mold. Refrigerate 6 to 8 hours.

Remove from mold by running a sharp knife around the edge and briefly dipping the bottom of the mold in hot water. Turn the mold over onto a chilled serving plate. Garnish with buttered nuts. Serves 8.

Daddy Charlie's Jamaican con Pollo

CHARLIE SAVAGE

½ cup olive oil or chicken fat
1 fryer, cut up in small pieces
1 teaspoon curry powder
1 teaspoon dried thyme
1 teaspoon dried oregano
1 tablespoon salt
1 tablespoon crushed red pepper flakes
1 cup coarsely chopped green bell pepper
1 cup coarsely chopped onion
1 cup coarsely chopped celery
3 cloves garlic, peeled and minced
3 bay leaves
3 cups white rice, unwashed
1 pound diced cooked ham or sausage (or 1 cup of each)
1 pound large shrimp, peeled and deveined
6 cups water
1½-ounce package Bijol (found in ethnic section of grocery stores)
1½-ounce package Goya Sazón, for color (found in ethnic section of grocery stores)
1 dozen cleaned, boiled blue crabs, split in half
1 cup black olives, sliced

Heat the olive oil or chicken fat until hot but not smoking in a large, heavy pot. Season the chicken with curry powder, thyme, oregano, salt, and red pepper flakes and brown on all sides in the hot oil; remove and set aside.

Cook the bell pepper, onion, celery, garlic, and bay leaves in the oil remaining in the pot until the vegetables are tender; stir into the chicken and set aside.

Brown the rice in the same pot and add to chicken.

Brown the sausage and/or ham and add to the chicken.

Cook the shrimp in the same pot until just beginning to turn pink; set aside separately from other ingredients. Return all other ingredients to the large pot.

Bring the water to a boil in another pot and add the Bijol and Sazón. Pour the water over all the ingredients in the large pot. Add the sliced olives. Add the boiled crabs and bring to a rolling boil; add the shrimp, stir, cover, and simmer on lowest heat for 30 minutes. Serves 12.

15

Where's the Beef?

Brookins Beef Stroganoff
Beef Stew
Oxtail Stew
Oxtail and Leek Stew
Camp Stew
Marie Sessions' Hamburger Combo Meal
Meatloaf Supreme
Japanese Cutlets
Fried Beef Liver

The only time to eat diet food is while you are waiting on the steak to cook.

JULIA CHILD

Mama has an iron frying pan with a lid that she bought new from Sears, Roebuck for ninety-eight cents when she and my daddy married in 1935. On Sundays Mama cooked roast beef; it was Daddy's favorite meat. She ruined several roasts before she invested a whole dollar in an iron frying pan. They had a wood stove, and she slow-cooked tender roast beef on the back burner, where the temperature was lower. By the time my two brothers and I were born (1943–1946), Mama and Daddy had a brand new house and, in time, they purchased an electric stove. By the time I noticed that old iron frying pan, it had acquired magical powers.

Whatever food Mama cooked in the iron frying pan turned out guaranteed good. This pan quickly became a cherished kitchen tool for all of our family. It was also one pot that wouldn't burn up. A long time ago, before the Kentucky Fried Chicken franchise, people fried chicken at home. In our home, we fried and smothered chicken, boiled cow tongue, and cooked roast beef and lots of other meats in the iron frying pan. The big iron frying pan was hauled into service every time we cooked a meal.

Melba Brookins (1935). Many fine homes that her father, Sanford Augustus Brookins, built after the turn of the century in Jacksonville are still standing.

We began our day frying bacon and eggs or pancakes and sausages. At dinnertime it was used to cook the meat. During the Thanksgiving and Christmas holidays, we used this pan to bake sweet potato pone. On payday, Daddy made chili in the old iron frying pan. When he cooked, all of us, including Mama, swarmed around him to fetch or chop at his command. Sometime during the latter part of the 1990s, I began to notice that my mama wasn't doing as much cooking as she had in times past. In 2003 she finally let me have her iron frying pan (I had been begging for it for years). Now I cook for Mama's house and mine using the magic iron frying pan every time.

Melba Brookins Sunday cooks beef Stroganoff the way her mama, Charlotte, did back when they had a wood stove. Melba's father, Sanford Augustus Brookins, was a master builder who came to Jacksonville in 1904 and during his career built over 500 fine homes, including some on American Beach. When his three children—Melba, Daisy, and Dykes—were in high school, he bought them cars. When they graduated from college and married, he built them homes. Melba shares this Brookins family favorite with us.

Brookins Beef Stroganoff

MELBA BROOKINS SUNDAY

1½ pounds beef shoulder or top round
1 tablespoon lemon juice
½ teaspoon salt
½ teaspoon coarsely ground pepper
4 tablespoons butter, margarine, or oil, divided
1 large onion, minced
½ teaspoon dried thyme
1 tablespoon cornstarch
½ teaspoon dry mustard
1 cup beef broth
½ cup sour cream
Cooked rice or noodles

Wash the beef and pat dry with paper towels. Cut it into strips about 2 inches long, 1 inch wide, and ¼ inch thick. Put the meat into a bowl and combine with the lemon juice, salt, and pepper. Let it sit, covered, for an hour at room temperature, stirring occasionally.

In a large skillet, melt 2 tablespoons butter, margarine, or oil and brown the meat quickly, in 2 batches, on all sides, adding some of the onion and thyme to each batch. Don't try to brown the meat strips and onion all at once. Remove the browned meat and onion from the skillet with a slotted spoon and keep hot, covered, on a platter placed over a pot of very hot water.

Stir the cornstarch and dry mustard into the cold broth until dissolved. Pour this mixture into the skillet and stir over medium heat, scraping up anything that is stuck to the pan. When the mixture starts to thicken, return the meat to the pan and stir well. Reduce the heat, add the sour cream, stir for about 1 minute, and serve over rice or noodles. Serves 4.

Bill Strain, formerly of Jacksonville, has been a fixture on American Beach from the beginning.

Beef Stew

WILLIAM "BILL" STRAIN

3 pounds beef short ribs
Salt and pepper
¼ cup all-purpose flour
2 tablespoons olive oil
1 quart water
1–2 large bay leaves
1 onion, coarsely chopped
2 tablespoons Worcestershire sauce

4 medium white potatoes, peeled and quartered
4–6 carrots, scraped and sliced in ¾- to 1-inch pieces

Season the beef ribs with salt and pepper to taste. Dredge in flour and shake off excess. Heat the olive oil in an iron pan until hot but not smoking. Sear the ribs on all sides in batches. Return all ribs to the pan and add the water, bay leaves, and onion. Bring to a boil, lower the heat, cover, and simmer for one hour. Add the Worcestershire sauce, potatoes, and carrots and cook covered for an additional 30 minutes, or until potatoes and carrots are tender. Serves 6.

Oxtail Stew

MIRIAM CUNNINGHAM BURNEY

2 pounds oxtails
1 small onion, diced
1 bay leaf
1 3½ cup can tomatoes
Salt and pepper
2 tablespoons all-purpose flour or cornstarch
6 tablespoons water

Place the oxtails in a stockpot and cover with water. Add onion and bay leaf and bring to a boil. Lower the heat and simmer covered 1½ hours. Add the tomatoes and salt and pepper to taste. Make a paste with the flour or cornstarch and water and add to the pot. Simmer covered 1 hour. Serves 4.

Oxtail and Leek Stew

MARSHA DEAN PHELTS

⅓ cup all-purpose flour
3 teaspoons salt, divided
1 tablespoon freshly ground pepper, divided
¼ cup oil
5 pounds oxtails
1 large onion, minced
1 large tomato, peeled and diced

1 large carrot, (to be discarded after oxtails become tender)peeled and quartered horizontally
2 cloves garlic, peeled and minced
Parsley sprigs (to be discarded after oxtails become tender)
1 bay leaf (to be discarded after oxtails become tender)
2 cans condensed beef broth
1 cup water
1 cup plus 2 tablespoons port
4 medium potatoes, peeled and quartered
1 pound carrots, scraped and sliced 1-inch thick pieces
1 bunch leeks, sliced 1-inch

Combine the flour with ½ salt and pepper. Dredge the oxtails in the flour mixture and shake off excess flour. In large Dutch oven heat oil until hot but not smoking. Brown the oxtails quickly on high, turning often; remove from pan. Drain the fat from the pan. Add the onion, tomato, carrot, garlic, parsley, bay leaf, beef broth, water, and 2 tablespoons port. Bring to a boil, reduce heat, cover, and simmer for 1½ hours, or until the oxtails are almost tender. Discard the carrot, parsley, and bay leaf and skim off the fat. Return the mixture to a boil, reduce the heat, and stir in the remaining port and salt and pepper. Simmer, covered, for 20 minutes. Add the potatoes and sliced carrots and simmer 10 minutes. Add the leeks and simmer up to 15 minutes, or until the leeks are tender. Remove the pot from the heat and allow meat to sit 10 minutes before serving. Serves 6–8.

~

Torrie Gilyard serves as a major partner in her family's catering and events enterprise.

Camp stew is an old recipe that Torrie Gilyard learned to cook from her father, Erving Gilyard, who had been cooking it since he was a child in the 1950s. Erving learned to make camp stew from an aunt, Ophelia Jacobs. It is quick and easy, and for generations the Gilyards have been sharing this hearty recipe with family and friends.

Camp Stew

TORRIE GILYARD

1 tablespoon olive oil
1 large onion, minced
1 clove garlic, peeled and minced
2 pounds lean ground beef
Salt and pepper
1 tablespoon dried parsley flakes
1 tablespoon fresh chives or 1 teaspoon dried
¼ teaspoon sugar
2 cans vegetable soup
Hot cooked rice

Heat the olive oil in a skillet until hot but not smoking. Sauté the onion and garlic until soft but not brown. Add the ground beef and brown. (If the ground beef has a lot of fat, remove the garlic and onion after sautéing. Brown the ground beef and drain off the fat. Return the meat to the skillet with the onion and garlic, then add the other ingredients.) Stir in salt and pepper to taste, parsley flakes, chives, and sugar, and simmer covered for about 2 minutes. Add the vegetable soup, mix well, and simmer covered for 10 to 15 minutes. Serve over hot rice. Serves 6.

Marie Sessions' Hamburger Combo Meal

MARIE SESSIONS

1 pound lean ground beef
½ teaspoon salt
1 teaspoon Worcestershire sauce
1 tablespoon freshly ground pepper
1 teaspoon dried oregano
1 teaspoon Italian seasoning
½ teaspoon minced garlic
1 medium onion, minced

Marie Sessions (*left*) and Grace Solomon take the oath of office as trustees of the American Beach Association, Inc. (1995).

1 16-ounce package frozen mixed vegetables, thawed
2 cups mashed potatoes
½ cup grated sharp cheddar cheese

Preheat oven to 350°.

Brown the ground beef. Stir in the salt, Worcestershire sauce, pepper, oregano, Italian seasoning, garlic, and onion. Drain the ground beef and spread evenly in the bottom of a 2-quart casserole dish. Spread the mixed vegetables over the ground beef and sprinkle with an additional half teaspoon of salt (optional). Evenly spread the mashed potatoes over the vegetables and bake for 35 minutes. Evenly spread the grated cheese over the potatoes and return to the oven for 5 minutes to melt the cheese. Serves 4.

Meatloaf Supreme

HARRIETT BAZZELL GRAHAM

1½ pounds ground beef
2 eggs, lightly beaten
3 tablespoons minced onion

2 teaspoons garlic salt
½ teaspoon pepper
¼ cup milk
1 8-ounce can tomatoes
2 tablespoons dried vegetable mix, such as Knorr Vegetable Recipe Mix
2 hard-boiled eggs, peeled

Preheat oven to 350°.

In a large bowl thoroughly mix all ingredients except hard-boiled eggs. Shape half of the mixture around each egg to cover completely. Place the meat loaves in an ovenproof dish and cover with foil. Bake for 30 minutes. Remove the foil and bake for 20 minutes. Serves 4.

Mr. & Mrs. John R. Graham
June 29, 1940

Afro-American Life Insurance Company employees Harriett Bazzell and John R. Graham (1940).

Japanese Cutlets

MARSHA DEAN PHELTS

4 medium-sized potatoes
½ pound lean ground beef
1 medium onion, minced
Salt and pepper
1 egg
1 cup fresh bread crumbs
Oil
Soy sauce
Catsup

Cover the potatoes with salted cold water by 2 inches, bring to a boil, lower the heat, and simmer until potatoes are just tender, 15 to 25 minutes. Peel and mash. Heat 2 to 3 inches oil in a skillet until hot but not smoking and brown the ground beef and onion. Add salt and pepper to taste. Combine the mashed potatoes and ground beef and form 6 patties.

Beat the egg in a shallow bowl and dip the patties in the beaten egg. Cover the patties with bread crumbs. Heat oil to 350° and deep-fry the patties until browned. Serve with soy sauce or catsup. Serves 6.

Fried Beef Liver

MARSHA DEAN PHELTS

2 pounds beef liver
Salt and pepper
1 cup all-purpose flour
2 large onions, sliced
½ cup oil, divided

Season the liver with salt and pepper to taste. Dredge in the flour and shake off excess flour. Heat 2 tablespoons of the oil in a skillet until hot but not smoking and sauté the onions until transparent. Remove the onions from the pan. Increase the heat to medium-high and pan fry the liver, approximately 5 minutes on each side. Return the onions to the skillet to warm. Serves 6.

16

Beach Breads

Cathead Biscuits
Drop Biscuits
Spoon Bread
Never–fail Rolls
Heavenly Cornbread
Broccoli Cornbread
Sylvia's Crackling Cornbread
Andy's Corn Fritter Casserole
Corn Fritters
Hoecakes
Jalapeño Hoecakes

A Jug of Wine, a Loaf of Bread—and Thou.

OMAR KHAYYAM

The Rosiers made their annual pilgrimage to American Beach the second weekend in July. From left, Kenny, Marsha, and Charles Jr. Our mama, Eva, is standing behind us (1957).

Biscuits were my little brother Kenny's favorite morsel, and our Aunt Liza kept him supplied with bags of them. When Aunt Liza invited the family over for a meal, she baked an extra cookie sheet of biscuits for Kenny. Our Aunt Eula, who lived in Sanford, Florida, did the same thing for Kenny whenever Daddy took us to Central Florida on freshwater fishing trips. Our family never knew what appeal little Kenny used to work these pans of biscuits for us, but he charmed a take-home sack every visit. My big brother Charles and I were equally delighted with Kenny's bounty because we ate these tasty morsels for days.

As a teenager Kenny worked at Harry's Drive-in Restaurant on U.S. 90 between McDuff and Canal streets. White customers were served in the main dining room; black truckers making runs had to use the backdoor entrance. Black truckers ate at a three-seat card table next to the kitchen sink—which is not the privileged location that five-star chefs treat lucky diners to.

From the cook at Harry's, Miss Eva Mae, Kenny learned to make cat-head biscuits. He figures the restaurant called the biscuits catheads because that's about the size of them, and they were soft and fluffy. Miss Eva Mae didn't measure ingredients; she simply poured and mixed until she got it just right. She taught Kenny how to make these biscuits. He continues to use a big soda water bottle for his rolling pen.

Cathead Biscuits

KENNETH ROSIER (KENNETH DIAAB MAHDI)

2½ cups all-purpose flour, divided	1 stick cold butter
3 teaspoons baking powder	1 egg, separated
½ teaspoon salt	1 cup milk
1 teaspoon sugar	

Preheat oven to 450°.

Combine 2 cups flour, the baking powder, salt, and sugar in a bowl. Cut in the butter with a fork until combined and mixture resembles coarse meal. Add the egg yolk and milk to the dough and stir. Turn the dough out onto a surface covered with ½ cup flour and knead a few times to form a ball. Roll dough to a half-inch thickness. Using a mayonnaise jar, press down on the dough with ¼-inch twists to cut biscuits out. Place the biscuits on a greased cookie sheet. Beat the egg white and brush the top of each biscuit. Bake for 15 to 20 minutes, or until golden brown. Makes 10–12.

Drop Biscuits

NELLIE RAGLAND HENRY

2 cups all-purpose flour	⅓ cup vegetable shortening
1 tablespoon baking powder	1 tablespoon mayonnaise
1 teaspoon salt	¾ cup milk

Preheat oven to 450°.

Mix the flour, baking powder, and salt. Cut in the shortening with a fork or two knives until crumbly. Add the milk, mayonnaise and mix only enough to wet the dry ingredients. Drop the dough from a tablespoon onto a greased baking sheet and bake 10 to 12 minutes, or until lightly browned. Makes 12.

Joseph Nathaniel Henry and his wife, Nellie. As a daring kid, Joe and his friends swam 1,500 yards out to the blue line, where the water changes color because of its depth.

Spoon Bread

ALEXANDER HICKSON

2 cups milk
1 cup plain cornmeal
4 tablespoons butter

½ teaspoon salt
3 eggs, well beaten
2 teaspoons baking powder

Preheat oven to 350°.

Scald the milk in a saucepan, then stir in the cornmeal, butter, and salt. Cool, then stir in the eggs and baking powder. Bake in a buttered 2-quart casserole dish for 25 minutes, or until a knife inserted in the center comes out clean. Serves 8.

Never-fail Rolls

LOIS ISZARD

1 package yeast
½ cup warm water

½ cup vegetable shortening
½ cup hot water

2 tablespoons sugar
1 teaspoon salt
1 egg, beaten

3 cups all-purpose flour
2 tablespoons melted butter

Sprinkle the yeast over ½ cup warm water and let stand until foamy. Soften the shortening in ½ cup hot water in a large mixer bowl, then stir in the sugar and salt. Add the egg and mix well. Stir in the flour and beat well with mixer; the dough will be soft. Turn the dough into another bowl, cover, and refrigerate overnight if possible. (Dough can be refrigerated for 3 or 4 days. Let rise 1 hour or more before baking.)

Preheat oven to 425°.

Turn the dough out onto a floured surface and knead well. Roll out ¼- to ½-inch thick and cut with 2-inch biscuit cutter. Brush with melted butter. (Or cut and fold over for pocketbook rolls.) Bake until brown, 10 to 15 minutes. Makes 2 dozen.

Heavenly Cornbread

WILLIE MAE HAYES

16 ounces sour cream
1 16-ounce can cream-style corn
1 16-ounce can whole kernel corn, drained

2 sticks margarine, melted
4 eggs, slightly beaten
2 packages corn muffin mix

Preheat oven to 300°.

Combine the ingredients in the order given. Pour into a greased 9-inch × 13-inch pan and bake for 50 to 55 minutes. Heavenly cornbread is a very moist, rich dish. Serves 6.

Broccoli Cornbread

LETONY SESSIONS

½ cup butter, melted
⅓ cup minced onion
1 teaspoon salt
¾ cup cottage cheese
8 ounces shredded cheddar cheese, divided

1 10-ounce package frozen chopped broccoli, thawed and drained
4 eggs, slightly beaten
1 package corn muffin mix

Preheat oven to 400°.

Combine the butter, onion, salt, cottage cheese, broccoli, and half of the shredded cheddar cheese in a bowl and stir with a spoon until blended. Stir in the eggs and corn muffin mix. Pour this mixture into a well-greased 9-inch × 13-inch casserole dish or an iron skillet. Sprinkle the remaining cheese evenly over the top and bake for 25 minutes, or until golden brown. Serves 6.

~

My schoolmate, college roommate, colleague, and lifelong neighbor in Jacksonville and on American Beach, Sylvia Jenkins Brown, personified a one-woman band. People loved being around her because she was always a party in full swing, whether she was alone (she seldom was) or in a group. She genuinely embraced people and gave wise council to multi-generational groups. In the summer, she taught cooking and sewing to the children in the community. When Sylvia cooked, the neighborhood would be fed. It was nothing out of the ordinary for her to cook a complete dinner for my husband and me and bring it over. Michael could wolf down a pot of greens at one sitting, and I could do likewise with her crackling cornbread. After hogging the cornbread and the greens, we both ate the remaining courses, including the dessert, more sensibly.

The last time that Sylvia brought us dinner, in the winter of 2005, I asked why her crackling cornbread was so good. The secret was that she made the cracklings tender by soaking them for five minutes in a cup of boiling water. I, along with hundreds of Sylvia's friends, were stunned upon learning that she had died of an aneurysm on March 4, 2005, less than a month before our spring fling on American Beach.

Sylvia's Crackling Cornbread

SYLVIA JENKINS BROWN

1 cup pork cracklings
1 egg
2 cups buttermilk (to make buttermilk, add 2 tablespoons vinegar or
    lemon to 2 cups whole milk and let sit 30 minutes)
2 cups cornmeal
¼ cup all-purpose flour
2 tablespoons sugar
1 teaspoon baking powder

1 teaspoon baking soda	¼ cup olive oil
1 teaspoon salt	3–4 hot peppers, minced

Preheat oven to 400°.

Soak the cracklings in boiling water to cover for 5 minutes and drain. Mix all ingredients and pour into a well-oiled 9-inch iron skillet. Bake for 20 minutes. Serves 8.

Andy's Corn Fritter Casserole

ANDREW B. COLEMAN III

3 tablespoons butter or margarine, softened
3 large egg whites, slightly beaten
8 ounces cream cheese, softened
½ cup minced onion
½ cup minced red bell pepper
1 16-ounce can whole kernel corn, drained
1 16-ounce can cream-style corn
1 8-ounce package corn muffin mix
Pepper to taste

Preheat oven to 375°.

Combine the butter or margarine, egg whites, and cream cheese in a large bowl and whisk until smooth. Stir in the onions, bell pepper, whole kernel corn, and cream-style corn and mix well. Add the corn muffin mix and pepper to taste, stirring well. Pour into a 7-inch × 11-inch casserole dish coated with vegetable oil. Bake for 50 to 60 minutes, or until a toothpick inserted in the center comes out clean. Serves 10.

Corn Fritters

MARSHA DEAN PHELTS

1 14.5-ounce can cream-style corn	½ cup milk
1 teaspoon salt	1½ cups cornmeal
¼ teaspoon pepper	½ cup all-purpose flour
1 egg, beaten	Additional oil for frying
1 teaspoon vegetable oil	

Heat oil to 360° to 370°.

Combine all ingredients. Drop by heaping teaspoons into hot fat; don't crowd. Brown both sides. Drain on paper towels. Makes 30.

Hoecakes

JOSEPH NATHANIEL HENRY

1½ cups cornmeal
½ teaspoon salt
½ teaspoon baking powder
1 cup water
4 tablespoons oil, divided

Combine the dry ingredients. Stir in the water and 2 tablespoons oil. Beat until mixed well. In an iron skillet heat the remaining oil until hot but not smoking. Drop the batter by tablespoonfuls into the skillet and cook until browned on both sides. Drain on paper towels. Makes 10–12.

Jalapeño Hoecakes

MARSHA DEAN PHELTS

1 cup cornmeal
¾ cup all-purpose flour
1½ teaspoons baking powder
½ teaspoon salt
1 cup buttermilk (to make buttermilk, add 2 tablespoons vinegar to whole milk)
4 tablespoons oil, divided
1 egg, beaten
2 jalapeño or other hot peppers, seeded and minced

Combine the dry ingredients. Add 2 tablespoons of oil and the remaining ingredients, mixing well with a wooden spoon. Consistency should be like that of hush puppy batter, moist and slightly stiff. Heat the remaining oil in an iron or other heavy frying pan until hot but not smoking. Drop batter in by heaping tablespoonfuls and fry until brown on both sides. Drain on paper towels. Makes 10–12.

17

Candy Kitchen

Peanut Butter Balls
Cream Cheese Mints
Homemade Butter Mints
Fudge
Toasted Almond Truffles
Pecan Bourbon Balls
Walnut Bourbon Balls
Brandy Balls
Strawberries in the Snow

'Tis an ill cook that cannot lick his own fingers.
WILLIAM SHAKESPEARE

While I am confident that I am recognized as a really good cook, there is no comparison between me and my friend Deloris Gilyard's culinary skills. Deloris runs circles around my meal preparations; she caters, decorates, and plans events on a grand scale. Her catering engagements take her all over the island and far beyond.

Deloris remembers first cooking for her siblings when she was seven, and her Big Mama let her try her hand at making a dinner of bacon, canned tomatoes, and gummy rice (because she used too much water). The response from her two brothers and two sisters encouraged Deloris to try even more meal planning. Deloris cooked all through school and college in the dormitories at Florida State University and for her Alpha Kappa Alpha sorority sisters.

Deloris enjoys a dual career as an award-winning high school teacher and an excellent caterer. She shares the results of her catering with her entire family and many of her American Beach neighbors. When I need a cooking tip, I go to Deloris before I go to my collection of vintage cookbooks. I happily tag along as her least-skilled helper on catering assignments so I can pick up pointers. Over the years, Deloris has called upon me to make dainty, homemade candy treats. I am good at chopping and rolling. Candy making on American Beach is a joy.

Back in the 1950s and the 1960s, a place called the Sweet Tooth was on the north side of the ramp leading to the ocean. It sold cotton candy and ice cream. The enormous structure that is still standing on the south side of the ramp is where the candy kitchen was set up. One day recently, while walking on the beach, Deloris and I entered the long-boarded-up Candy Kitchen. To our joy, we found a handful of candy catalogs.

Peanut Butter Balls

DELORIS GILYARD

1 16-ounce jar peanut butter (smooth or crunchy)
1½ sticks margarine or butter, softened
2 tablespoons vanilla extract
1 16-ounce box confectioners' sugar, sifted
16 ounces dark or white chocolate
1 cup golden raisins, optional
Rum, optional

Combine the peanut butter and margarine or butter. Gradually add the vanilla and confectioners' sugar, stirring until combined. Shape the mixture into 1-inch balls. Refrigerate 1 hour.

Melt the chocolate in a double boiler on top of the stove or in a microwave according to package directions of chocolate. Dip the peanut butter balls in chocolate and place on wax paper–lined cookie sheets. Makes 120 pieces.

You may halve or quarter this recipe. I make this quantity to avoid measuring peanut butter and confectioners' sugar.

Optional: Marinate 1 cup golden raisins in rum to cover overnight. Drain the raisins and stir into peanut butter mixture. Continue as directed above.

~

Of the mint recipes, I find that one is just as good as another. It simply depends on the ingredients that you have on hand—cream cheese or whipping cream and butter. These homemade mints are wonderful treats.

Cream Cheese Mints

DELORIS GILYARD

3 ounces cream cheese, room temperature
2½ cups confectioners' sugar, sifted
5–6 drops oil of peppermint extract (found in health food stores or with spices in grocery stores)
Few drops food coloring, any color you choose
½ cup superfine sugar

In a large mixing bowl, beat the cream cheese with an electric mixer until soft. Gradually beat in the 2½ cups confectioners' sugar. Dust a wax paper–covered cutting board with superfine sugar, pour the cream cheese mixture onto the cutting board, and knead to a consistency that is smooth, not sticky. Add the peppermint extract and food coloring.

Roll out the dough to a ¼-inch thickness. Use a 1-inch spice bottle or other cutter to cut the mints. Place the mints on a wax paper–lined cookie sheet to harden for 12 hours at room temperature. Turn the mints over and allow to sit at least 12 hours until bottoms are hard. Store in refrigerator in an airtight container. Makes 4 dozen.

Homemade Butter Mints

MARSHA DEAN PHELTS

¼ cup whipping cream
1 pound confectioners' sugar, sifted
1 tablespoon unsalted butter, softened
5–6 drops pure peppermint oil (health food store) or pure peppermint
   extract (McCormick's)
Drop of green food coloring
½ teaspoon salt

Pour the cream into a mixing bowl. Add the confectioners' sugar very slowly, stirring with a spoon. Add the butter, peppermint oil, and food coloring. Mix thoroughly, then knead with hands until well mixed and creamy. Roll out on a cutting board to a ¼-inch thickness. Use a 1-inch cutter or bottle to cut the mints. You may choose to hand roll these mints in to ¼-inch balls. Allow to dry 3 or 4 hours at room temperature before storing in container. Makes 4 dozen.

Variation: For orange-flavored butter mints, use a drop each of red and yellow food coloring, 1 teaspoon orange extract, and ½ teaspoon grated orange peel.

Fudge

MARVIN ROOKS

4 heaping tablespoons unsweetened cocoa powder
3 cups sugar
⅓ cup light corn syrup
1 cup milk
Salt
1 stick butter or margarine
1 teaspoon vanilla extract
1 cup nuts

Mix the cocoa and sugar well in a 2½-quart heavy saucepan. Stir in the corn syrup, milk, and a dash of salt and mix well. Bring the mixture to a boil, then reduce heat to medium-high and cook without stirring until candy reaches the soft-ball stage, 235° (or until a drop of the candy forms a soft ball when dropped into cold water). Remove from heat and pour into a mixing bowl. Add the butter or margarine and vanilla. Beat with an electric mixer on high until the candy sticks to a spoon or feels a little grainy. Add nuts and pour into a 9-inch × 13-inch pan or a large platter. Makes 12–16 pieces.

The trick is to cook it just right and to beat it just right. It may take a little practice.

Toasted Almond Truffles

MARSHA DEAN PHELTS

½ cup canned evaporated milk
¼ cup sugar
1¾ cups (11.5-ounce package) semisweet chocolate morsels
½ teaspoon almond extract
½ teaspoon vanilla extract
1 cup finely chopped toasted almonds

Combine the milk and sugar in a small, heavy saucepan. Bring to a full rolling boil over medium-low heat, stirring constantly. Boil, stirring constantly, for 3 minutes. Remove from heat. Stir in the chocolate. Stir vigorously until the mixture is smooth. Stir in almond and vanilla extracts. Refrigerate for 2 hours.

Shape into 1-inch balls and roll in nuts. Refrigerate in airtight container until ready to serve. Makes 24 pieces.

Pecan Bourbon Balls

MARSHA DEAN PHELTS

2½ cups vanilla wafer crumbs (a 12-ounce box yields 4 cups of crumbs)
1 cup confectioners' sugar, sifted
1 cup coarsely chopped pecans
⅓ cup bourbon
¼ cup light corn syrup
1 8-ounce chocolate bar for cooking

In a large bowl combine the cookie crumbs with the sugar and pecans and stir until thoroughly mixed. In a small bowl combine the bourbon and corn syrup, then stir into the crumb mixture until completely blended. Shape the mixture into 1-inch balls and refrigerate about 1 hour, or until firm.

Chocolate Coating:

Melt the chocolate in a small, heavy saucepan over very low heat, stirring constantly until smooth. Using a long metal skewer or toothpicks, dip each bourbon ball into the melted chocolate to coat. Set aside on wax paper until chocolate is firmly set. Store in a tightly covered container in the refrigerator for up to 2 weeks. Makes about 5 dozen party-delectable morsels.

Walnut Bourbon Balls

EVELYN GREEN JEFFERSON

About 5 dozen packaged vanilla wafers, finely crushed (2½ cups)
2 tablespoons unsweetened cocoa powder
1 cup sifted confectioners' sugar plus additional for dusting
1 cup chopped walnuts, or a combination of walnuts and flaked coconut
3 tablespoons light corn syrup
¼ cup bourbon

Combine the crumbs, cocoa, 1 cup confectioners' sugar, and walnuts (or walnut-coconut mix). Add the corn syrup and bourbon; mix well. Shape into 1-inch balls and roll in confectioners' sugar. Store in a covered container a day or so to ripen; these keep very well. Makes 5 dozen.

Brandy Balls

EVELYN GREEN JEFFERSON

1 14-ounce box vanilla wafers, finely crushed
½ cup honey
⅓ cup brandy
⅓ cup light rum
1 pound walnuts, chopped
Granulated sugar

In a bowl mix the cookie crumbs, honey, brandy, rum, and walnuts. Shape into bite-sized balls and roll in granulated sugar. Place in an airtight container to seal the flavors. Keeps fresh for two weeks. Serve in a brandy snifter or clear fish bowl. Makes 5 dozen.

Strawberries in the Snow

MARSHA DEAN PHELTS

8 ounces white chocolate (vanilla, almond, or chocolate cooking bars
3 pints fresh strawberries
Round toothpicks
Styrofoam cylinder or block

Melt the chocolate according to package directions on the stove or in the microwave. Wash the strawberries and pat dry. Dip each strawberry into the melted chocolate and place on wax paper–lined cookie sheets. If chocolate becomes too thick while dipping, add a little melted vegetable shortening until it reaches the right consistency. Do not soften chocolate with anything but melted vegetable shortening; butter, oil, milk, or water will ruin this chocolate.

I enjoy serving strawberries in the snow at Christmastime. This is as close as I want to be to snow in Florida. Chocolate-covered strawberries are a tasty treat anytime you can get good fruit and are extremely easy to make. At Christmas, I arrange them on a 12-inch × 4½-inch Styrofoam cone. At Easter, I serve them in a straw or ceramic basket, and other times they are set in pastel paper baking cups and arranged on a crystal platter.

Use fresh strawberries with the leaves still attached. I have discovered that the toothpick is the key to maintaining the symmetrical shape of the strawberries. Insert round wooden toothpicks in the middle of the strawberry's base. With your fingers, pull the leaves toward the center and hold against the toothpick. Dip the strawberry in melted chocolate. Shake excess chocolate back into the container, hold the strawberry upright, and insert the exposed end of the toothpick into a sturdy piece of Styrofoam. Save Styrofoam packaging blocks to use for holding strawberries on toothpick while chocolate hardens. Makes 36–45.

18

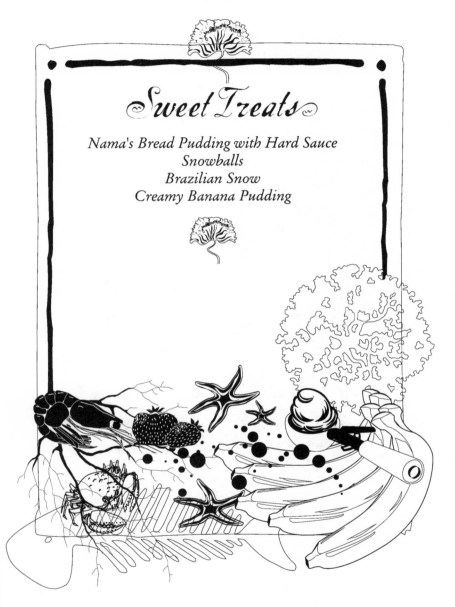

Sweet Treats

Nama's Bread Pudding with Hard Sauce
Snowballs
Brazilian Snow
Creamy Banana Pudding

Sweets for the sweet is my principle.
WILLIAM SHAKESPEARE

Carrot cakes are Mr. Natural's signature dish, but it is his Nama's bread pudding and the hard sauce that we crave most. Dennis Stewart learned to cook by following his grandmother Marie Stewart around the kitchen of her beach cottage when he was a little boy. Dennis observed the ever-present pint bottle of Christian Brothers brandy that she kept in the icebox. Little Dennis thought that Nama had the whiskey bottle there for taking a sip; he was wrong. As he grew older and helped more often in the kitchen, he discovered that this bottle of Christian Brothers brandy served as the powerful kick in Nama's bread pudding.

The Stewarts. Seated, Ralph Sr. with David. Standing, from left, Dennis, Marie (Nama), and Ralph Jr. (1935).

Dennis Stewart Jr. (*left*), and Michael, in the early 1950s.

The family now calls on Mr. Natural to serve up this treat from the hilltop cottage on American Beach that he shares with Nama's grandchildren. Nama's spirit lives in the cottage, and her bread pudding can't be eaten in silence. People holler praises from the first mouthful to the last swallow. So good it is, so good.

Nama's Bread Pudding with Hard Sauce

DENNIS STEWART (MR. NATURAL)

1 loaf French bread, 1 or 2 days old
1½ cups sugar
4 teaspoons ground cinnamon
6 eggs, beaten
3 cups of canned evaporated milk

½ cup raisins
½ cup shredded coconut
½ cup chopped nuts
1 teaspoon vanilla extract
1½ sticks butter or margarine, melted

Preheat oven to 325°.

In a large mixing bowl, break the bread into pieces and sprinkle with enough water to cover. Set aside to soak.

In another bowl, combine the sugar, cinnamon, and eggs. Beat gently until the mixture is smooth. Add the evaporated milk, raisins, coconut, nuts, and vanilla and stir until well blended. Squeeze the water from the bread and add to the mixture, folding bread in gently until well mixed. Add the melted butter or margarine and fold in gently. Pour the mixture into a lightly greased 8-inch × 11-inch baking pan and bake 25 minutes. Serves 12.

Hard Sauce:

1 stick butter or margarine, softened
¼ cup firmly packed light brown sugar
¼ cup brandy
½ teaspoon vanilla extract
¼ teaspoon freshly grated nutmeg
1 teaspoon fresh lemon juice
Whipped cream

Mix all ingredients until smooth. Refrigerate until a hard paste is formed.

To serve, spoon 1 teaspoon hard sauce over a serving of hot bread pudding, add a dollop of fresh whipped cream, and you will see Nama as you holler.

Snowballs

EVELYN GREEN JEFFERSON

1 quart vanilla or pistachio ice cream
1 cup flaked coconut
4 ounces Midori liqueur, divided

4 green maraschino cherries, optional
2 ounces coffee bean candy, optional

Roll 4 scoops vanilla or pistachio ice cream into balls. Coat each with flaked coconut, put on a cookie sheet in a single layer, and place in the freezer.

When ready to serve, place coconut-covered ice cream balls in individual serving dishes. Drizzle 2 tablespoons Midori liqueur over each ball. Garnish with green maraschino cherries or coffee bean candy. Serves 4.

Brazilian Snow

MARSHA DEAN PHELTS

⅓ cup freshly roasted coffee beans
1 quart French vanilla ice cream, softened slightly
Whipped cream
4 maraschino cherries

No more than 5 minutes before serving, grind the coffee beans as finely as possible; reserve 1 tablespoon. Sprinkle one-third of remaining coffee over the ice cream in the carton. With an ice cream scoop, scoop out one layer of ice cream and place in an individual serving dish, mixing coffee and ice cream together as much as possible without overhandling or coloring the ice cream. Repeat 3 times. Top each serving with whipped cream and sprinkle with a little of the reserved ground coffee. Garnish with cherries and serve immediately. Serves 4.

Creamy Banana Pudding

LOIS ISZARD

1 14-ounce can sweetened condensed milk
1½ cups cold water
1 4-serving size instant vanilla flavor pudding and pie filling
1 pint whipping cream, whipped
36 vanilla wafers
3 bananas, sliced and dipped in lemon juice

In a large bowl, combine the condensed milk and water. Add the pudding mix and beat well. Chill 5 minutes. Fold in the whipped cream.

Spoon pudding mixture into a 2½-quart glass serving bowl or 8 individual serving dishes. Top with one-third each of the wafers, bananas, and remaining pudding. Repeat twice, ending with pudding. Chill thoroughly. Garnish as desired. Serves 8.

19

Cakes

American Beach Flag Cake
Red Velvet Cake
Nama's Sour Cream Surprise Cake
Cream Cheese Pound Cake
Coconut Pound Cake
Carrot Cake
Hummingbird Cake
Punch Bowl Cake
Bourbon Pecan Cake
Baby Food Plum Cake and Glaze
Brown Sugar Cake
Big Mama's Fruitcake
Age–old American Beach Fruitcake
White Fruitcake

Pat-a-cake, pat-a-cake, baker's man, bake me a cake as fast as you can.
MOTHER GOOSE

Amerian Beach has come into its own as an art colony, along with the rest of Amelia Island. Many performing and visual artists find the island irresistible and, like countless others, carve out their niches alongside natives. On American Beach Alexander Hickson opens his rustic southwestern-motif home as a summer retreat for theatrical readings and poetic expressions. Hickson, a teacher, singer, dancer, and actor, coaches and directs a group of islanders by selecting plays and making weekly reading assignments. He affords locals opportunities to discuss plays and read with professionals who drop by for an evening of enchantment.

The natural landscaping of his oceanfront lawn is an ideal amphitheater. Here the seaward dunes serve as a backdrop and as a privacy wall from those strolling along the shore. At the base of the dunes is a sunken orchestra pit, hollowed out by Hurricane Dora in 1964. Alexander's yard and patio serve as a natural stage. In front of the stage is the deck where guests sit on benches built along the outer walls, reading, rehearsing, discussing, and waiting for their cue. The evening heightens; the sounds of bongos played by Rod Starling, dual resident of Jacksonville and New

Marsha Dean Phelts on a Sunday afternoon at Evans' Rendezvous (1972).

York, rise from the orchestra pit. As the beat from Rod's drums floats out to the sea, the sounds travel across Ocean Boulevard and waft their way fifty feet upward to the top of Nana, the highest dune on Amelia Island. The sound of tambourines joins the beat of the bongos. Our bodies move, bob, snap, and dance in synchronization with native rhythms.

As the readings run into the night, the troupe rushes inside to plunge into a smorgasbord of creative delicacies prepared and displayed by participants. If the group numbers twelve, at least a dozen dishes compete for consumption and praise. When the group numbers twenty-four, we roar. We eat heartily and drink merrily. Corks pop. Bubbles rise, and the sweet fruits of champagne flow through the night in sparkling stemware.

Readings on the Fourth of July are unparalleled and by far the most festive of the summer theater. Spectacular fireworks from the Ritz-Carlton to the north and Amelia Island Plantation to the south light up the night skies over the ocean for more than an hour. At Alexander's we sit in a valley between dunes to the east and west, watching waves and blazing fireworks from the north and south rushing to the shore, and we extol the blessings of life on an enchanted American Beach—so beautiful.

American Beach Flag Cake

ALEXANDER HICKSON

2 pints fresh strawberries
1½ cups boiling water
1 8-serving size package
    strawberry- or cherry-flavored
    gelatin
1 cup cold water
1 12-ounce pound cake,
    cut into 10 slices
1⅓ cups fresh blueberries, divided
8-ounce tub whipped topping

Slice 1 cup of the strawberries; halve the remaining strawberries.

Stir the boiling water into the gelatin in a bowl and stir until completely dissolved. Mix the cold water and enough ice to make 2 cups. Stir into the gelatin until the ice is melted. Refrigerate 5 minutes, or until slightly thickened.

Line an 8-inch × 12-inch dish with cake slices. Stir the sliced strawberries and 1 cup blueberries into the gelatin. Spoon evenly over the cake. Refrigerate 4 hours, or until firm. Spread the whipped topping over the gelatin. Arrange strawberry halves and remaining blueberries on top to create a flag. Serves 16.

Red Velvet Cake

SHELIA WALKER

½ cup butter
1½ cups sugar
2 eggs
2 ounces red food coloring
2 tablespoons unsweetened
  cocoa powder
1 teaspoon salt

2¼ cups all-purpose flour
1 cup buttermilk (to make
  buttermilk, add 2 tablespoons
  vinegar to whole milk)
1 teaspoon vanilla extract
1 teaspoon baking soda
1 tablespoon vinegar

Preheat oven to 350°.

Cream together the butter, sugar, and eggs. Make a paste with the red food coloring and the cocoa, blending well, then add to the creamed mixture. Add the salt, flour, buttermilk, and vanilla. Slowly add the baking soda and vinegar until well blended. Pour the mixture into 2 well-greased 8-inch cake pans. Bake for 30 minutes. Prepare frosting while layers cool. Serves 15.

White Frosting:

¼ cup butter, softened
2 cups confectioners' sugar, sifted
2 tablespoons cream

1 teaspoon lemon juice
1 teaspoon vanilla extract

Place all ingredients in a small bowl and beat with an electric mixer on the lowest speed until well blended. Beat on high speed until smooth and creamy. If needed, add a little more cream to thin.

After frosting the red velvet cake you may garnish with coconut flakes and pecan halves.

Nama's Sour Cream Surprise Cake

MICHAEL STEWART

3 cups all-purpose flour
¼ teaspoon salt
¼ teaspoon baking soda
1 cup butter, softened
3 cups sugar

6 eggs
1 cup sour cream
¼ teaspoon vanilla extract
Pecans to cover bottom of tube pan
1 teaspoon ground nutmeg or mace

Preheat oven to 300°.

Combine the flour, salt, and baking soda. Set aside. Cream the butter and sugar until creamy. Add one egg at a time, beating well after addition. Stir in vanilla. In a large bowl, alternately add small amounts of dry ingredients, creamed mixture, and sour cream, beginning and ending with dry ingredients.

Grease a tube cake pan and spread pecans on the bottom. Spoon the cake batter over the pecans and sprinkle with nutmeg or mace. Bake for 1½ hours. Remove from pan immediately and cool on a wire rack.

Don't be surprised that you've never baked a cake as tasty as sour cream surprise pound cake. Serves 15.

Cream Cheese Pound Cake

LOIS ISZARD

3 sticks butter, softened
8 ounces cream cheese, softened
3 cups sugar
6 eggs

3 cups sifted cake flour
1 teaspoon vanilla extract
1 teaspoon almond extract

Preheat oven to 325°.

In a large bowl cream the butter and cream cheese until smooth. Add the sugar and stir until fluffy. Add eggs one at a time, blending well after each addition. Add the cake flour to the creamed mixture and combine well. Stir in vanilla and almond extracts. Pour the batter into a 12-inch greased tube pan and bake for 1½ hours. Cool in the pan on a wire rack 10 minutes, then remove from the pan and continue cooling on the rack. Serves 15.

Coconut Pound Cake

CARUTHER (RUTH) GODWIN

2 sticks butter, softened
1 stick margarine, softened
8 ounces cream cheese, softened
3 cups sugar
6 eggs

3 cups all-purpose flour
2 tablespoons cold water
2 teaspoons coconut flavoring
1 4-ounce can coconut flakes

Cream the butter, margarine, and cream cheese until smooth. Add the sugar slowly, beating well after each addition. Add eggs one at a time, beating well after each addition. Add the flour slowly to the creamed mixture and blend well. Stir in the cold water, coconut flavoring, and coconut flakes. Pour into a well-greased and floured tube pan. Place in a cold oven and cook at 325° for 1½ hours, or until a toothpick inserted in the center comes out clean. Serves 15.

Carrot Cake

NINA WATSON

1¼ cups oil	1 teaspoon salt
2 cups sugar	4 eggs
2 cups sifted flour	3½ cups grated carrots
2 teaspoons baking powder	1 cup raisins
2 teaspoons ground cinnamon	1 cup chopped nuts
1 teaspoon baking soda	

Preheat oven to 325°.

Combine the oil and sugar and mix well. Sift together the dry ingredients. Sift half of the dry ingredients into the sugar mixture and blend. Sift in remaining dry ingredient alternately with eggs, one at a time, mixing well after each addition. Stir in carrots and nuts until well blended. Pour into lightly oiled 10-inch tube pan. Bake about 1 hour and 10 minutes. Cool upright in the pan on a wire rack. Serves 15.

Note: It works best to bake in 3 layers.

Icing:

8 ounces cream cheese, softened
½ stick butter or margarine, softened
1 box confectioners' sugar, sifted
1 teaspoon vanilla extract
2 tablespoons cream or milk, if needed
1 cup chopped nuts

Mix all ingredients except the nuts. Cream well and then stir in the nuts. Frost cake top(s) when completely cool.

Hummingbird Cake

LOIS ISZARD

3 cups all-purpose flour
2 cups sugar
1 teaspoon baking soda
1 teaspoon salt
1 teaspoon ground cinnamon
1 cup chopped pecans, walnuts,
    or almonds

3 eggs, lightly beaten
1½ cups corn oil
1 teaspoon vanilla or almond extract
2 cups chopped firm ripe bananas
1 20-ounce can crushed pineapple,
    undrained

Preheat oven to 325°.

Mix the flour, sugar, baking soda, salt, and cinnamon in a large bowl; stir in the nuts. Combine the eggs with the oil, extract, bananas, and pineapple with juice. Add to the dry ingredients and mix thoroughly by hand. Spoon into a well-oiled 10-inch tube pan.

Bake for 1 hour and 20–25 minutes. Cool in the pan 10 to 15 minutes, then invert onto a wire rack. Cool completely before frosting. Serves 15.

Frosting:

8 ounces cream cheese, softened
1 pound confectioners' sugar, sifted
1 stick butter or margarine

Mix all ingredients with an electric mixer until smooth.

Punch Bowl Cake

MARSHA DEAN PHELTS

1 yellow cake mix
1 5.1 ounce package instant vanilla pudding, prepared according to
    package directions
1 21-ounce can cherry pie filling
1 16-ounce can fruit cocktail, drained
1 20-ounce can crushed pineapple, drained
1 14-ounce bag coconut
2 12-ounce containers frozen whipped topping, thawed
2 cups chopped nuts no need to toast

Bake a 2-layer cake according to package directions. Cool completely on wire racks.

Crumble one of the cake layers into the bottom of a punch bowl. Spoon in half of the pudding, half of the cherry pie filling, half of the fruit cocktail, half of the pineapple, half of the coconut, a container of whipped topping, and half of the nuts. Repeat. Refrigerate until chilled and ready to serve. Serves 36.

Bourbon Pecan Cake

CARUTHER (RUTH) GODWIN

½ cup raisins
¼ cup bourbon
¾ cup butter or margarine, softened
2 cups firmly packed light brown sugar
4 eggs
2½ cups all-purpose flour
1 teaspoon baking soda
1 teaspoon baking powder
1 teaspoon ground nutmeg
1 cup buttermilk (to make buttermilk, add 2 tablespoons vinegar to whole milk)
2 cups chopped pecans no need to toast

Preheat oven to 350°.

Grease and flour a 10-inch tube pan. Soak the raisins for 30 minutes in the bourbon. Cream the butter or margarine and the brown sugar until smooth. Add eggs one at a time, beating well after each addition. Combine the flour, baking soda, baking powder, and nutmeg. Add the dry ingredients to the creamed mixture alternately with the buttermilk, blending well after each addition. Stir in the pecans and drained raisins. Turn into the prepared pan and bake for 50 minutes, or until a cake tester inserted in the middle comes out clean. Cool on a wire rack for 15 minutes. Loosen the cake with spatula; turn out topside up to cool completely. Drizzle the cake with brown drizzle, then white drizzle. Serves 15.

Brown Drizzle:

3 tablespoons butter or margarine
½ cup firmly packed light brown sugar

3 tablespoons heavy cream
⅓ cup chopped pecans

Melt the butter or margarine in a small pan. Stir in the brown sugar and heat until the sugar dissolves and the mixture bubbles. Add the heavy cream and heat 1 minute. Add the nuts and heat until bubbly. Cool slightly.

White Drizzle:

2 tablespoons hot milk
1 cup confectioners' sugar, sifted

⅓ cup chopped pecans
Few drops bourbon

Combine the milk and confectioners' sugar. Stir in the nuts. Add bourbon until the mixture is the proper consistency for drizzling.

Baby Food Plum Cake and Glaze

CARUTHER (RUTH) GODWIN

2 cups self-rising flour
2 cups sugar
1 cup oil
3 eggs

1 teaspoon vanilla extract
1 cup chopped pecans
2 small jars plum baby food

Preheat oven to 350°.

Combine all ingredients well. Pour into a greased and floured 10-inch tube pan and bake 1 hour, or until a toothpick inserted in the center comes out clean. The cake may be removed from the pan while hot. Glaze while hot. Serves 15.

Glaze:

1 cup confectioners' sugar, sifted
3 tablespoons lemon juice

Mix confectioners' sugar and lemon juice and drizzle over hot cake.

Brown Sugar Cake

CARUTHER (RUTH) GODWIN

¾ cup butter or margarine, softened
¼ cup vegetable shortening
1 cup granulated sugar
2 cups firmly packed light brown sugar

2 teaspoons vanilla extract	½ teaspoon salt
6 eggs	1 cup canned evaporated milk
3⅓ cups sifted cake flour	1 cup flaked coconut
½ teaspoon baking powder	1 cup chopped nuts

Preheat oven to 325°.

Cream the butter or margarine and shortening in a large bowl; gradually add the granulated sugar and brown sugar and beat until light and fluffy. Blend in the vanilla. Add eggs one at a time, beating well after each addition.

Sift together the flour, baking powder, and salt. Add to the creamed mixture alternately with the evaporated milk and beginning and ending with the dry ingredients. Mix well; fold in the coconut and nuts. Pour into a well-greased and floured 10-inch tube pan. Bake approximately 1 hour 35 minutes, or until a toothpick inserted in the center comes out clean. Cool on a wire rack. Serves 15.

Glaze:

⅓ cup butter or margarine
1 cup firmly packed light brown sugar
¼ cup canned evaporated milk
1 teaspoon vanilla extract

Melt the butter or margarine in a saucepan over medium heat. Add the sugar and stir until dissolved. Add the milk and bring to a rolling boil. Boil 2 minutes. Cool. Add the vanilla to the cooled glaze and beat until it reaches spreading consistency. Drizzle over the cake. Or you may choose simply to dust the cake with powdered sugar. Good! Good! Good!

∾

This recipe has been handed down for over 90 years, at least as far back as 1914, the year Mama was born. It was a staple on Big Mama Agnes Cobb's Christmas dinner menu, right along with the collard greens, baked hen, ambrosia, and other delights that nobody cooked better than she did. Big Mama died in 1980, and Vera, her youngest of six, wrote this old recipe down in 1942, when she married Joseph Gibson. My whole life I had enjoyed this succulent, dark, and moist fruitcake swaddled in brandy-saturated cheesecloth and kept in a cake tin in a dark closet until ripe. Then, Christmas of 1999, my Aunt Vera gave me my fruitcake along with her recipe and her cake pans. Vera told me that this was the last fruitcake she

Aunt Vera, my mama's baby sister, preserved Big Mama's fruitcake recipe for posterity (1940).

would bake and if I wanted any more, I'd have to bake them for myself. The day after Christmas, I was at the grocery store looking for candied fruits and nuts that might be on sale.

Big Mama's Fruitcake

VERA COBB GIBSON

4 sticks butter or margarine, softened
3 cups firmly packed light brown sugar
8 eggs
5 cups all-purpose flour, divided
5 teaspoons baking powder, divided
1 cup milk
2 teaspoons vanilla extract
2 teaspoons black walnut extract
6 cups mixed nuts, including pecans, Brazil nuts, and English walnuts, cleaned

1 pound candied fruit mix
1 27-ounce jar mincemeat

Preheat oven to 275°.

Cream the butter or margarine and brown sugar. Add the eggs and combine well. Add 4 cups of the flour, 1 cup at a time, and 4 teaspoons baking powder, beating well after each addition. Stir in the milk and vanilla and black walnut extracts.

Dredge the fruit and nuts in the remaining cup of flour and add to the mincemeat. Blend well and add to the creamed mixture. Stir well with your hands gloved or with a large and strong wooden spoon.

Pour the mixture into a well-greased or parchment-lined tube pan and bake for 3 hours. Use any leftover batter for baking a sampler (smaller-sized) fruitcake. Serves 25.

Age-old American Beach Fruitcake

JOYCE ROBINSON

2 cups candied fruit
2 cups white raisins
1 pint dark rum or bourbon
2 cups butter or margarine, softened
1 pound firmly packed dark brown sugar
2 cups granulated sugar
8 eggs, separated
4 cups chopped pecans
5 cups sifted all-purpose flour, divided
4 teaspoons ground nutmeg
1½ teaspoons salt
4 teaspoons baking powder
Dark rum or bourbon for cheesecloth

Combine the candied fruit, raisins, and rum or bourbon in a bowl. Cover tightly and refrigerate overnight. Drain and reserve liquid.

Preheat oven to 275°.

Place the butter or margarine in a large mixing bowl and beat on medium speed until light and fluffy. Add the brown and granulated sugars gradually, beating well after each addition. Add the egg yolks and blend well.

Joyce and James Robinson have made many civic contributions to the community.

Dredge the pecans in a half cup of flour and set aside. Combine the remaining flour, nutmeg, salt, and baking powder in a separate bowl. Add 2 cups of the flour mixture to the creamed mixture; mix thoroughly, gradually adding fruit-soaking liquid. Gradually add remaining flour, beating well after each addition.

Beat the egg whites until stiff but not dry. Fold them gently into the batter. Add the drained fruit and pecans and blend thoroughly.

Grease a 10-inch tube pan and line it with wax paper or parchment paper. Grease and flour the paper lightly. Pour the cake batter to 1 inch from the top of the pan. Pour the remaining batter in a loaf pan prepared the same way.

Bake the tube pan 2 ½ to 3 hours, or until a toothpick inserted in the center comes out clean. Bake the loaf pan 2 hours, or until a toothpick inserted in the center comes out clean.

Cool the cakes in the pans on a wire rack for 2 to 3 hours, then remove from the pans and pull off the paper liner. Wrap the cakes in cheesecloth soaked in dark rum or bourbon. Wrap the cheesecloth-covered cakes in aluminum foil and store at least 2 weeks in an airtight container in the refrigerator. Serves 20.

Over the years, Lois Iszard has been making thank-yous for colleagues from the kitchen of her cottage on the ocean and delivering them to the doors of recipients. A thank-you note from the Iszards at Christmas can be a whole cake. Lois is organized and can pump out tasty dishes frequently and effortlessly.

White Fruitcake

LOIS ISZARD

1 pound candied pineapple
1 pound candied cherries
2 cups all-purpose flour
2 sticks butter, softened
1 cup sugar
5 eggs, beaten
2 tablespoons vanilla extract
2 tablespoons lemon extract
4 cups nuts

Preheat oven to 300°.

Dredge the fruit and nuts in the flour in a large bowl. Cream the butter, sugar, and eggs. Stir in the vanilla and lemon flavoring. Combine the creamed mixture with the fruit and nuts. Pour in 10-inch tube cake pan, greased and floured. Bake 2 hours or until a toothpick inserted in the center comes out clean. This cake can be frozen for up to a year. Serves 20.

20

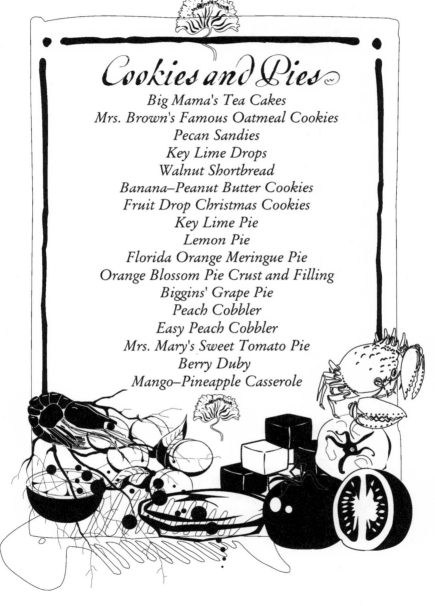

Cookies and Pies

Big Mama's Tea Cakes
Mrs. Brown's Famous Oatmeal Cookies
Pecan Sandies
Key Lime Drops
Walnut Shortbread
Banana–Peanut Butter Cookies
Fruit Drop Christmas Cookies
Key Lime Pie
Lemon Pie
Florida Orange Meringue Pie
Orange Blossom Pie Crust and Filling
Biggins' Grape Pie
Peach Cobbler
Easy Peach Cobbler
Mrs. Mary's Sweet Tomato Pie
Berry Duby
Mango–Pineapple Casserole

Promises and pie crust are made to be broken.
JONATHAN SWIFT

B y no means were Big Mama's tea cakes my favorite cookies during childhood; nevertheless, I ate them from a brown paper bag practically every time I went over to her house. In her large and welcoming home, tea cakes were as much a staple as were coffee, grits, rice, cornmeal, or flour. They were always there for us children and any of Big Mama's company who wanted something sweet during the week. It didn't require much effort or many ingredients to make the tea cakes, so Big Mama made them big, thick, and in enormous batches that didn't run out. Every week, she supplied these semisweet treats to the teachers at Isaiah Blocker Elementary School, where Aunt Pearlie taught.

My friend Deloris, who grew up in Bronson, a small town near the Gulf Coast of Florida, remembers trading sandwiches, fruits, and other items from her lunch with a classmate each day for a tea cake. Not me—I was ashamed to be seen with a tea cake in my brown lunch bag and wouldn't dare take those hard cookies to school.

On weekends, Big Mama baked rich pound cakes, sour cream cakes, or coconut cakes. She baked and cooked with butter rather than margarine. According to Big Mama, margarine was no substitute for butter in anything. I use butter in this recipe only because Big Mama put it in hers. I feel certain that margarine would do just as well, but my Big Mama swore by butter; it was an absolute for her.

Big Mama's Tea Cakes

AGNES LLOYD COBB

1 cup firmly packed light brown
    sugar (or more if you need it)
1 cup unsalted butter
2 eggs, beaten
¼ cup maple syrup
3 cups all-purpose flour

1½ teaspoons baking soda
1 teaspoon ground cinnamon
1 teaspoon ground ginger
1 teaspoon ground nutmeg
½ teaspoon salt

Cream the sugar and butter well. Stir in the eggs and syrup. Combine the flour and spices and slowly add to the creamed mixture, stirring well after each addition. Chill 30 minutes. Clean utensils, put things away items, and get cookie sheets ready.

Preheat oven to 350°.

Remove the dough from the refrigerator, knead until smooth, and roll to ½-inch thickness. Use a 2½-inch cookie cutter or glass to cut out the tea cakes. Place the cookies on an ungreased cookie sheet 2 inches apart. Bake 10 minutes. Makes 2½–3 dozen.

Mrs. Brown's Famous Oatmeal Cookies

ELVIRA GIBSON BROWN

2 eggs
1 cup vegetable shortening
1 cup firmly packed light brown
    sugar
1 cup granulated sugar
1 teaspoon baking soda
½ teaspoon salt

1 cup all-purpose flour
1 cup flaked coconut
2 cups quick-cooking oatmeal
1 cup chopped black walnuts
1 cup baking raisins (or raisins that
    have been soaked in water at
    least 1 hour before using)

Beat the eggs slightly in a large bowl. Add the shortening and sugars and blend. Add the baking soda, salt, and flour and blend well. Add the coconut, oatmeal, walnuts, and raisins and combine well. Refrigerate 4 hours, or overnight.

Preheat oven to 350°.

Drop dough by the teaspoonful on a greased cookie sheet and bake 10 to 12 minutes. Makes 3 dozen.

Pecan Sandies

MARSHA DEAN PHELTS

1 cup butter or margarine, softened
⅓ cup sugar
2 teaspoons water
2 teaspoons vanilla extract

2 cups all-purpose flour, sifted
1 cup chopped pecans
Confectioners' sugar

Cream the butter or margarine and sugar. Add the water and vanilla and mix well. Stir in the flour and pecans and chill dough 3 to 4 hours.

Preheat oven to 325°.

Shape the dough in 1-inch balls or crescents. Place 1 inch apart on an ungreased cookie sheet and bake about 20 minutes. Cool slightly, then roll in confectioners' sugar. Makes 5 dozen.

I usually shake one or two at a time gently in a small bag with the confectioners' sugar in it. If I am feeling really ambitious, I shake them again after they are completely cooled. The second coat is more even in appearance.

Key Lime Drops

MARSHA DEAN PHELTS

Key Lime Drops Topping:

2 teaspoons grated lime peel
1 cup sugar
⅓ cup lime juice

Mix the ingredients for the topping before mixing the cookies. Let stand. Spoon on the topping while the cookies are hot.

Cookies:

1½ cups sugar
¾ cup vegetable shortening
2 eggs
1½ teaspoons grated lime or lemon peel
3 cups all-purpose flour
½ teaspoon baking soda
2 teaspoons baking powder
1 teaspoon salt
1 cup sour cream
2 teaspoons lime extract
¾ cup macadamia nuts
½ cup white chocolate chips

Preheat oven to 375°.

Cream together the sugar, shortening, and eggs. Sift together the flour, baking soda, baking powder, and salt. Add the lime peel and dry ingredients to the creamed mixture. Add the sour cream and lime extract and mix well. Stir in the nuts and white chocolate chips and blend well. Drop 1 inch apart by teaspoonfuls on greased cookie sheets and bake 12–15 minutes. Makes 5 dozen.

Walnut Shortbread

EVELYN GREEN JEFFERSON

2 cups all-purpose flour, sifted
¼ teaspoon baking powder
¼ teaspoon salt
1 cup butter or margarine, softened
⅔ cup firmly packed light brown sugar
¾ cup chopped walnuts
Cinnamon-sugar
Walnut halves

Preheat oven to 300°.

Combine all ingredients except cinnamon-sugar and roll out on a lightly floured surface to ¼-inch thickness. Cut the dough into diamonds, squares, triangles, and circles. Place 1 inch apart on ungreased cookie sheets. Sprinkle with cinnamon-sugar and decorate with walnut halves. Bake 20 to 30 minutes. Makes 3 dozen.

Banana–Peanut Butter Cookies

HARRIS TEETER GROCERY

1½ cups all-purpose flour
½ teaspoon baking soda
1 small ripe banana, mashed (about ½ cup)
⅓ cup firmly packed light brown sugar
¼ cup soft margarine spread
¼ cup creamy or chunky reduced-fat peanut butter spread
1 large egg
1 teaspoon vanilla extract

Preheat oven to 375°.

Combine the flour and baking soda in a small bowl. In a medium mixing bowl, beat together the banana, brown sugar, margarine spread, and peanut butter spread until light and fluffy, using an electric mixer on medium speed. Beat in the egg and vanilla. Gradually beat in the flour mixture until a dough forms. Shape the dough into 1-inch balls and place 2 inches apart on baking sheets sprayed with vegetable cooking spray. Using the tines of a fork dipped in flour, press a crisscross pattern onto each cookie. Bake until edges are set, about 10 minutes. Place baking sheets on wire racks and cool for about 5 minutes. Makes about 45 cookies.

Fruit Drop Christmas Cookies

NORMA LEUTHOLD

1 stick butter or margarine, softened
1½ cups firmly packed light brown sugar
4 eggs
3 scant teaspoons baking soda
3 tablespoons milk
3 cups plus 2 tablespoons all-purpose flour, unsifted
½ cup bourbon, or more
1 teaspoon ground allspice
1 teaspoon ground cinnamon
1 teaspoon ground cloves
1 teaspoon ground nutmeg
2 pounds red candied cherries
1 pound green candied pineapple
3 pounds pecans

Preheat oven to 300°.

Cream the butter or margarine and brown sugar. One at a time, beat eggs lightly and add to creamed mixture, mixing well after each addition. Mix the baking soda and milk and add to the mixture, stirring well. Add the flour, bourbon, and spices and combine well. Dredge the fruit in 2 tablespoons flour and combine with the pecans; add to the dough and stir gently. Drop scant teaspoonfuls 1-inch apart on greased cookie sheets. Bake 20 to 25 minutes. Makes about 12 dozen.

Key Lime Pie

ALEXANDER HICKSON

3 eggs, separated
1 can sweetened condensed milk
¾ cup fresh key lime juice

1 pie shell baked in 9-inch pie pan
6 tablespoons sugar

Preheat oven to 425°.

In the bowl of an electric mixer, beat the egg yolks and condensed milk until combined; add the lime juice and mix until smooth. Pour the uncooked filling into the baked pie shell. Beat the egg whites on high until they begin to hold their shape, then gradually beat in the sugar until meringue holds stiff peaks. Spoon the meringue over the filling and seal to pastry edge. Bake 5 to 7 minutes, or until meringue is golden. Allow the pie to cool, then refrigerate 2 hours. At this point, a most tasty key lime pie is ready for serving. Serves 8.

Lemon Pie

EMMA HOLLEY MORGAN

1 cup sugar
3 tablespoons cornstarch
1 tablespoon grated lemon peel
¼ cup butter or margarine
¼ cup fresh lemon juice
1 cup milk
3 egg yolks, slightly beaten
1 cup sour cream
1 baked 9-inch pie shell
Whipped cream, optional

In a saucepan, combine the sugar, cornstarch, lemon peel, butter or margarine, lemon juice, milk, and egg yolks. Cook over medium heat, stirring constantly, until thick. Place a piece of plastic wrap directly on the surface of the pie filling and cool. Fold in the sour cream and pour into the baked pie shell. Chill at least 2 hours before serving. Top with whipped cream or you may choose to use the three egg whites to make a meringue. Serves 8.

Meringue:

3 egg whites
6 tablespoons sugar

Beat the egg whites on high until stiff, gradually adding sugar while beating. Spread the meringue over the cooled pie and seal to pastry edge. Broil 7 minutes, or until meringue is golden; or bake in a 450° oven for 10 minutes, or until meringue is golden.

Florida Orange Meringue Pie

MARSHA DEAN PHELTS

1 cup fresh orange juice
1 cup orange sections, cut in pieces
2 tablespoons grated orange peel
1 cup sugar
5 tablespoons cornstarch

3 egg yolks, beaten
2 tablespoons lemon juice
2 tablespoons butter or margarine
1 baked 9-inch pie shell

Preheat oven to 450°.

Combine the orange juice, orange pieces, orange peel, sugar, and cornstarch in a saucepan and cook on low heat until clear. Add some of the hot mixture to the egg yolks, stirring constantly. Stir yolks into the hot mixture and cook about 5 minutes longer. Remove from heat. Blend in the lemon juice and butter or margarine. Pour into the baked pie shell. Be sure filling and shell are both hot or both cold. Cover the filling with meringue and seal to pastry edge (see p. 227 for a meringue recipe). Bake until meringue is lightly browned.

Orange Blossom Piecrust and Filling

MARSHA DEAN PHELTS

Piecrust:
1½ cups fine gingersnap crumbs
¼ cup butter, softened
1 tablespoon grated orange rind

Preheat oven to 325°.

Mix all ingredients well and press firmly into a 9-inch pie plate. Bake for 8 minutes. Maintain oven temperature.

Pie Filling:

1 envelope unflavored gelatin
¼ cup cold water
3 eggs, separated
½ cup sugar, divided
1 6-ounce can frozen orange juice concentrate, thawed
1 tablespoon lemon juice.

Soften the gelatin in the cold water for 5 minutes. Beat the egg yolks. Cook the yolks, ¼ cup sugar, orange juice, and lemon juice in a double boiler over simmering water, stirring constantly, until mixture thickens, approximately 5 minutes. Add the gelatin to the egg yolk mixture and cool. Pour the cooled filling over the piecrust.

Beat the egg whites until stiff, adding 1 teaspoon of remaining sugar at a time. Spread the meringue over the cooled filling and seal to pastry edge. Return the pie to the oven and brown the meringue slightly. Refrigerate and serve chilled. Serves 8.

~

Nick Biggins lives in Cleveland Heights, Ohio, now. Growing up, Nick lived down the road from American Beach, in Alachua County, in the north central section of the state. Nick vividly remembers the thrilling trips to American Beach from his childhood home in Waldo. Waldo was then, and still is, a small country town outside of Gainesville and is most noted for being a speed trap as listed by the American Automobile Association. In the 1950s Nick and his friends came to American Beach at night to race their cars on the beach to see how fast they could go.

American Beach continued to attract Nick and his friends. When he returned from the army, Nick almost settled on American Beach. He sometimes wonders what his life would have been like if he had. He shared the family recipe for grape pie with me.

From spring through summer, mulberries, blackberries, grapes, and pears grow wild on American Beach and all over Amelia Island. Berry pickers and cooks stop by the roadside and on abandoned properties to pick berries and grapes by the gallon. When the grapes climb, crawl, and drop all over American Beach and Amelia Island at the end of summer, my grandson, Kurt, and I set up a taste-test kitchen at the beach house and cook up grapes for show and tell and giveaway treats.

Norris Biggins (*left*) with his cousins Maxine Dimps and Otis Green (early 1950s).

Biggins' Grape Pie

NORRIS "NICK" BIGGINS

2 pounds concord grapes
¼ cup water
1 cup sugar
3 tablespoons tapioca
1 tablespoon lemon juice
Salt
1 tablespoon unsalted butter or margarine
2 unbaked 9-inch pie shells

Preheat oven to 425°.

Stem the grapes and wash. Measure 4 cups of grapes and remove the skins; set the skins aside. Cook the grape pulp with the water for 10 minutes. Rub the pulp through a sieve to remove seeds. Combine the skins, sieved pulp, sugar, tapioca, lemon juice, and a pinch of salt. Line a 9-inch pie plate with 1 piecrust. Add the filling and top with the second crust. Place the pie on a cookie sheet and bake 45 minutes. Serves 8.

Peach Cobbler

PEARLIE SCARBOROUGH

1 gallon can sliced peaches, drained
⅓ cup all-purpose flour or ¼ cup cornstarch
½ cup water, approximately
2½ cups sugar
½ cup honey
2 teaspoons ground nutmeg
2 teaspoons vanilla extract
Yellow food coloring
2 sticks butter or margarine, divided
4 unbaked 9-inch pie shells

Cut the sliced peaches in half. Mix the flour or cornstarch with enough water to make a smooth paste. In a large pot cook the peaches, sugar, honey, nutmeg, vanilla, a few drops of food coloring, and 1 stick butter or margarine over medium heat until the butter melts. Stir in the flour or cornstarch paste to thicken the filling. When the filling has thickened and begins to bubble, remove the pan from the heat.

Cover the bottom of a 9-inch × 13-inch glass baking dish with a layer of peaches. Quarter 2 pie shells and place evenly over the peaches. Slice the remaining stick of butter or margarine and dot half over the crust. Broil until the crust browns, approximately 15 minutes. Remove the baking dish from oven and repeat layering. Broil until the crust browns, approximately 15 minutes. Remove from the oven cool before serving. Serves 10.

This recipe from noted writer Dori Sanders is different from the peach cobblers to which I have become accustomed. I was skeptical about trying it, but after assurances from a fellow librarian, Arden Brugger, I did. It is absolutely wonderful and truly easy.

Easy Peach Cobbler

DORI SANDERS

1¼ pounds firm, ripe peaches (5–6 medium)
1 tablespoon fresh lemon juice

1⅔ cups sugar, divided
1 stick unsalted butter, melted
1 cup all-purpose flour
1 tablespoon baking powder
¼ teaspoon salt
1 cup whole milk
Ground cinnamon or nutmeg, optional

Put the oven rack in the middle position and preheat oven to 375°.

Cut an X in the bottom of each peach with a sharp paring knife and blanch peaches, in 2 batches, in a 3-quart saucepan of boiling water 10 seconds. Transfer the peaches with a slotted spoon to a bowl of ice water. Peel off the skin with a paring knife, beginning from the scored end, and discard. Halve the peaches, then pit and cut lengthwise into ¼-inch slices.

Transfer the peaches to a heavy 3-quart saucepan and add the lemon juice and ⅔ cup sugar. Bring to a boil over high heat, stirring constantly, and boil, stirring occasionally, 4 minutes. Remove from heat.

Pour the melted butter into a 9-inch × 13-inch baking dish. Whisk together the flour, baking powder, salt, and remaining cup of sugar in a bowl, then whisk in the milk until just combined. Pour the batter over the melted butter (do not stir). Sprinkle lightly with cinnamon or nutmeg if desired and bake until the cobbler is bubbling and top is golden brown, 40 to 45 minutes. Cool on a rack 25 minutes. Serves 8.

Mrs. Mary's Sweet Tomato Pie

MARY STEWART

2 unbaked 9-inch pie shells
6 ripe tomatoes, each cut in 8 wedges
3 cups sugar
½ cup cornstarch
½ teaspoon ground cinnamon
¼ teaspoon ground ginger
½ cup lemon juice
1 tablespoon freshly grated orange peel or 1 teaspoon dried grated orange peel
4 tablespoons butter or margarine, melted, plus more for brushing pie shell

Salt
1 teaspoon cinnamon-sugar

Preheat oven to 350°.

Place 1 pie shell in an ungreased 9-inch deep-dish pie plate; press firmly along bottom and sides and trim excess crust from edges. Bake 10 minutes. Remove from oven and set aside to cool.

Blanch the tomatoes and remove the skin. Combine the peeled tomatoes, sugar, cornstarch, cinnamon, ginger, lemon juice, orange peel, 4 tablespoons melted butter or margarine, and a pinch of salt in a saucepan. Bring the mixture to a boil, lower heat, and simmer uncovered for 15 minutes. Spoon the cooked tomatoes over the baked pie shell. Top with the second pie shell and seal to pastry edge. Brush lightly with the butter and prick with a fork in several places. Sprinkle with cinnamon-sugar. Bake 40 minutes, or until crust is golden brown. Serves 8.

Berry Duby

VELMA STEWART

2 quarts freshly picked mulberries or blueberries
1 stick butter or margarine
2 cups sugar, or less according to taste
1 teaspoon vanilla extract
1 teaspoon ground cinnamon
1 teaspoon ground nutmeg

Clean and stem the berries. Place in a saucepan with water to cover by 1 inch and cook over medium heat for 20 minutes. Add the butter or margarine, sugar, vanilla extract, cinnamon, and nutmeg and set aside while preparing the dumplings.

Dumplings:

⅓ cup water or milk, approximately
1½ cups all-purpose flour

Stir the water or milk into the flour until blended. Dumpling batter should be stiff, not runny.

Bring the berries to a simmer. Drop the dumplings in by the teaspoonful and simmer 20 minutes, or until the dumplings pop to the top of the pot. Serves 8.

∼

Mangos are best eaten ripe from the tree, with nothing between teeth and tongue but the fruit. An abundance of these fruits may be preserved a while longer by making them into pies. Slice ripened mangos, flash freeze, then store in plastic freezer bags until ready to make pies. Jellies and ice cream may also be made, but to keep the purest taste of the delicious mango intact, eat them with all your heart from the peel or baked in a pie.

Mango-Pineapple Casserole

MARSHA DEAN PHELTS

2 unbaked 9-inch pie shells
4 large Florida-grown mangos, sliced, or 32-ounce jar sliced mangos, juice reserved
1 fresh pineapple, sliced, or 20-ounce can pineapple chunks, juice reserved
2 tablespoons cornstarch
1 cup sugar
1 teaspoon ground cinnamon
Juice of 1 lemon or lime
4 tablespoons butter or margarine

Preheat oven to 400°.

Line a buttered 2-quart, 2-inch deep casserole dish with a pie shell. Bake 5 minutes, or until lightly browned. Cool. Reduce oven temperature to 350°.

Cut fruit into bite-sized chunks. In a saucepan mix 2 cups juice from the mangos and pineapple with the cornstarch, sugar, and cinnamon (if you don't have enough juice from the fruit, supplement with a fruit nectar). Bring to a boil and remove from heat. Layer the fruit in the baked pie shell. Squeeze lemon or lime juice over the fruit and dot with butter. Pour the fruit juice over the filling and top with the second pie shell. Bake 45 minutes. Serves 8.

21

American Beach Jellies

The Beach Lady's Citrus Marmalade
The Beach Lady's Blackberry Jelly
The Beach Lady's Mulberry Jam
How to Make Grape Jelly
Grape Jelly
Grandma Betsch's Prickly Pear Cactus Jelly
American Beach Plum Jelly

*Getting the most from the least and living peacefully in harmony
with nature is the most rewarding lifestyle.*

MAVYNNE "THE BEACH LADY" BETSCH

merican Beach and Amelia Island's at one time most celebrated resident, Mavynne Betsch, born January 1935, died on Labor Day in 2005. Mavynne, a.k.a. the Beach Lady, made jam or jelly in every season. She had no need for a calendar to determine a season or a clock to learn the time of day. She recognized seasons by the flora and the fauna. She could accurately tell time within an hour by looking to the heavens. A vegetarian, the Beach Lady was known for musing, "I don't eat anything that has eyes." Throughout the year, she gathered wild berries and fruits to make jelly and juice.

The Betsch siblings on American Beach: Mavynne, John Jr., and Johnnetta (1949).

On American Beach, the making of jam and jelly is a seasonal thing that begins in the middle of winter, just after the holiday baking. Winter, like an elusive and free-spirited lover, comes and goes as it teases and flirts, here one day, but gone the next. The coldest spells last no longer than two or three days. After the first frost, citrus fruits are picked and shared throughout the neighborhood. When we get the warning of a freeze, surplus citrus is harvested and used in a festive cornucopia of preserves, marmalades, jams, candied peels, and zest. The Beach Lady had her pick among the orange, grapefruit, kumquat, tangerine, and lemon trees nestled in Deloris and Ervin Gilyard's orchard.

Schoolchildren glowed as they made their rounds gathering fruits to present to the Beach Lady upon her visit to a classroom.

Note

These jam and jelly recipes are not to be doubled when preparing. If for any reason a batch does not jell, do not attempt to reliquefy but, rather, use as syrup for pancakes or topping over ice cream sundaes.

The Beach Lady's Citrus Marmalade

2 grapefruits
2 large oranges
2 lemons
15 cups water
10½ cups sugar, warmed in oven for 15 minutes

Sterilize canning jars and lids and set aside.

Wash fruit skins well to remove any wax. Peel the fruit into ¼-inch-wide or smaller strips, being careful to avoid the white pith. Juice the fruits, strain, and set the juice aside. Remove pulp and seeds from the strainer, scrape pulp and pith from hulls, and pack in cheesecloth. Place peels in a 10-quart stainless steel stockpot. Add water and juices squeezed from citrus, place bag of pulp on top, and bring to a rolling boil. Lower heat and simmer for 30 minutes, or until mixture has reduced by one-third.

Use a large spoon or tongs to squeeze liquids from cheesecloth or jelly bag back into the pot, then discard the bag. For every cup of juice, use 1 cup warmed sugar (the sugar is warmed to speed up dissolving). Add sugar to the peel and juice mixture. Stir over low heat until the sugar has dissolved. Bring to a rapid boil and boil without stirring for 20 minutes, or until the marmalade reaches 220°. Remove the pot from the heat and skim off any foam. Let the marmalade sit a few minutes, or until a thin skin forms. Pour the marmalade into hot sterilized jars and seal tightly. Shake the jars gently as marmalade sets to distribute the peels. Makes 5 pints.

~

In spring burnt amber–tipped blackberry vines creep from their covers in the brush. Flocks of Carolina wrens returning to the north make an overnight stop for refueling on ripening berries and plump insects. Around the second week in May (Mother's Day), we try to gather more than the birds, selecting the juiciest deep-purple mulberries. Mulberries are used for making pies, dubys, and jams.

All too soon, spring transforms into summer without warning or notice except for the ripening of the blackberries and the frequent sightings of William Watson's breed of feral-domesticated bobcats foraging in the north dunes, where they feast upon tasty slender young snakes.

As summer approached and the red heads of blackberries burst through the brush, the Beach Lady alerted known jelly makers to the locations where these coveted fruits could be found.

The Beach Lady's Blackberry Jelly

2 quarts blackberries
1 cup water
Juice of 1 lemon
7 cups sugar, divided
1 1.75 ounce package fruit pectin

Sterilize eight ½-pint canning jars and lids and set aside.

Wash the berries and remove the stems. Place the berries in a large stainless steel stockpot and crush. Add the water and lemon juice, fruit pectin and bring to a boil over high heat. Reduce the heat and simmer 5 minutes. Strain and measure out 1 quart of juice.

In a heavy pot add the juice to the sugar and mix well. Bring to a rolling boil, stirring constantly. Skim off any foam. Pour the jelly into hot sterilized canning jars. Seal tightly.

The Beach Lady's Mulberry Jam

2 quarts mulberries
Juice of ½ lemon
1 1.75 ounce package fruit pectin
1 teaspoon butter or margarine
7 cups sugar

Sterilize 8 ½-pint canning jars and lids and set aside.

Wash the mulberries and remove stems. Place the berries in a large stainless steel stockpot and crush. Add water to cover, lemon juice, pectin, and butter or margarine. Bring to a rapid boil, stirring constantly. Add the sugar and return to a rolling boil, stirring constantly, and boil a full minute after sugar has dissolved. Remove the pot from the heat and pour the mixture in hot sterilized jars. Seal tightly. Makes 7 cups.

When my grandson, Kurt, comes to the beach, it seems as though we are on a marathon camping expedition; our days don't end until well past midnight. And though the trip from Jacksonville is less than forty minutes, we've never gotten to the beach in under four hours. Our first stop is at the nearest McDonalds's or country-breakfast restaurant. After a lei-

My grandson, Kurt Dean, in the kitchen mashing grapes that he gathered.

Kurt had to stand on a chair to pour sugar into the pot for making a batch of grape jelly.

surely breakfast, we head out on State Road 105 northeast for the thirty-mile drive to American Beach. A little over halfway to the beach, we drive past the Mayport Ferry Slip. We take a rest stop to look at the vast cargo ships in the channel inching their way to the mouth of the sea.

After watching the vessels in the channel, we board the ferry and ride (out of our way) just to see what is on the south side of the channel. We get a whiff of shrimp and other seafood being brought to the markets. We take a close-up look at the shrimp boats and the casino boats still at the docks, and then ride back across on the ferry and continue our journey. We drive to downtown Fernandina to the Wal-Mart for provisions, then at last—home to American Beach.

I follow Kurt sixty feet above sea level to the peek of Nana, Florida's tallest dune; from there Kurt surveys the island to determine our next foraging expedition. As we near the top, I lag behind to call for help for him if he needs it, because the west side of the dune does not slope to the other side. Much to my amazement, it drops sixty feet into a maritime forest.

When Kurt comes to the beach for Labor Day, he gets to make jelly from the wild grapes he picks from fences and trees. This is his recipe.

How to Make Grape Jelly

KURT ELIJAH DEAN

The first thing that you do is pick a lot of grapes [3 quarts]. Wash them very good then take the stems off all the grapes. Crush the grapes with a bottle. [Kurt uses a soda bottle or a bottled hot sauce bottle.] Put all of the grapes in a big pot and add 1 cup of water. Boil for 10 minutes. This makes 7 cups of grape juice. Add 7 cups of sugar and boil for 1 minute. Pour this into 8 little [sterilized] jelly jars.

∼

The making of grape jelly on American Beach is a sure sign of summer's end and fall's beginning. In seemingly no time, summer seeps into fall as easily as the first full kiss of spring months earlier shoved winter down under.

This basic recipe was taken from the *Twentieth Century Cook Book: A Feast of Good Things; a Careful Compilation of Tried and Approved*. This book was published in 1912 as a fund-raising project of the Deaconess Board of Bethel Baptist Institutional Church in Jacksonville. Mrs. Mary Frances Sammis Lewis was president of the Deaconess Board. She was the wife of A. L. Lewis and died in 1923, before the founding of American Beach and the birth of their great-granddaughter, Mavynne Betsch.

Grape Jelly

Put on the stove grapes just beginning to turn [ripen], boil, place in a jelly bag, and let drain. To 1 pint of juice add 1 pint of sugar and boil 20 minutes. As a general rule, allow equal measure of juice and sugar. Boil juice rapidly 10 minutes, skim, and add sugar. Boil 10 minutes longer. To test jelly, drop a little in a glass of very cold water and if it immediately falls to the bottom, it is done.

∼

In the fall the delicate and beautiful yellow roses of the prickly pear cactus wilt and the plant darkens, making the fruit ready for harvesting. The prickly pear cactus is handled gingerly. Its spines are removed carefully, and the pulp from its leaves is extracted for juice. These succulent plants grow undisturbed all over the beach dunes.

Over the years, Mavynne shared fond childhood memories of the prickly pear cactus jelly that her paternal grandmother, Mattie Betsch,

Prickly pear plants, from which Grandma Betsch used to make jelly, continue to grow all over the community.

made. This was the only grandmother that she knew. Grandma Betsch, while vacationing on American Beach from her home in Washington, D.C., gathered fruit to make her grandchildren sweet treats from the sandy beach.

Grandma Betsch's Prickly Pear Cactus Jelly

MATTIE BETSCH

Carefully pick prickly pear cactus fruits or purchase them in grocery stores. Use thick gloves or newspapers to handle.

6–8 prickly pear cactus fruits
7 cups sugar
1 teaspoon butter or margarine
Juice of 1 lemon
1 bottle liquid pectin
Drop or two of food coloring

Sterilize ½-pint canning jars and lids and set aside.

Remove as many spines from the fruit as possible. Place the fruit in a pan of boiling water for 1 minute. Remove from water and peel off skin.

Cut the fruit up and place in a clean pan of enough boiling water to cover. Cook for about 15 minutes. Pour through a cheesecloth to get 1 quart of juice.

Mix the juice, sugar, butter or margarine, and lemon juice. Bring to a rolling boil. Pour in the liquid pectin and return to a rolling boil for 1 minute. Add a drop or two of red, yellow, or green food coloring. Remove from heat, skim, and pour into hot sterilized canning jars. Makes 7 cups.

⁓

Our beach plums are ready for harvesting in August, when shrubs burst into a profusion of fruit. The plums linger on branches until they drop to the ground in their ripeness. Because of their tartness, children in the community have no use for them. But as we do with any surplus, we create uses for the bounty.

American Beach Plum Jelly

MARSHA DEAN PHELTS

3½ pounds beach plums
1½ cups water
Juice of 1 lemon
1.75 ounce package fruit pectin
1 teaspoon butter or margarine
7 cups sugar

Sterilize ½-pint canning jars and lids and set aside.

Clean the beach plums, pit and remove the stems. Place the fruit in a heavy stockpot and crush. Add the water and bring to a boil. Reduce heat, cover, and simmer 30 minutes. Use a metal strainer or colander to pour off juice, mashing softened fruit to extract juices.

Pour 5½ cups of strained beach plum juice and the lemon juice into saucepan and stir in the fruit pectin. Add the butter and bring mixture to a full rolling boil, stirring constantly. Add the sugar to the rapidly boiling beach plum juice and boil for 1 full minute. Skim foam with a metal spoon.

Fill sterilized canning jars within ⅛ inch of the top. Seal tightly. Makes 8 cups.

22

Pickling & Preserving Surplus on Cannery Row

Watermelon Rind Pickles
Okra Dill Pickles
Marinated Cucumbers
Herbed Olives
Marinated Mushrooms
Pickled Eggs
Corn Relish
Pickled Peaches
Preserved Kumquats

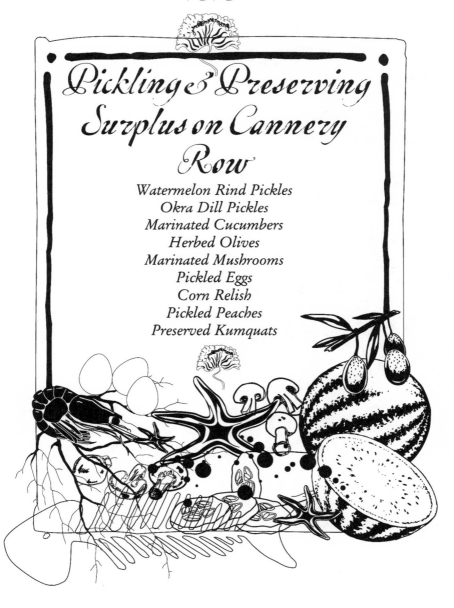

Food is life. And the way we lived, life was gathering, growing, and preparing food.
SALLY ANN ROBINSON

In her time, Mama preserved and canned vast amounts of produce from our garden (1935).

The art of canning is a practice that is hard to let go in this community. When there exists an abundance of backyard produce or a bunch of produce, preserving these bumper crops can be noticed throughout the community. In this community, people cook in season or buy on sale and find ways to preserve the surplus. I have fond memories of canning time in the kitchen, for this activity calls for all hands available. We stored our preserves in Mama's washhouse in the backyard.

Bottling the brilliant colors and tastes of garden produce at its peak is a year-round reward. My mama loves to pickle watermelon rinds. Her wide-eyed grandchildren accept her canned goods and preserves and wonder what to do with them. The pickled watermelon rinds are great on hamburgers and as relishes with pork or beef entrées.

Watermelon Rind Pickles

EVA R. LAMAR

3 pounds green watermelon rind
2 cups sugar
2 cups white vinegar
6 3-inch cinnamon sticks
2 tablespoons whole allspice
2 tablespoons whole cloves

Sterilize 3 pint-size canning jars and lids and set aside.

Cut the rind in 1-inch squares. Be sure that all the pink has been removed; you want only the rind. Soak overnight in water salted with 3 tablespoons of salt to each quart of water. After soaking, drain and cover with fresh water.

Cook the rinds until tender, approximately 25 minutes, and drain. Bring the sugar and vinegar to a boil; add the spices tied in a cheesecloth bag and the rind. Cook, uncovered, until liquid is transparent, approximately 45 minutes. Remove the spice bag. Pack the rind tightly in hot sterilized jars, pouring syrup to ⅛ inch from the top. Make sure that all of the rind is covered with hot liquid. Seal at once. Makes 3 pints.

Okra Dill Pickles

EVA R. LAMAR

3 pounds young stemmed whole okra, left whole
Leaves from one bunch celery
6 garlic cloves, peeled
6 bunches fresh dill, or 6 teaspoons dill seed
1 quart water
1 pint white vinegar (must be white)
½ cup salt
6 sterilized pint-size canning jars

Into each sterile pint jar pack cleaned uncut okra along with a few celery leaves, 1 clove garlic, 1 teaspoon dill seed or 1 bunch dill.

Mix the water, vinegar, and salt to make a brine. Bring to a boil. Pour the brine over the okra. Seal the jars. To process, place sealed jars in tepid water and bring to boil for twenty minutes. Remove from heat. Let jars stand 3 to 4 weeks to age. Chill before serving. Makes 6 jars.

Marinated Cucumbers

EVA R. LAMAR

2 unpeeled cucumbers, thinly sliced
½ cup cider vinegar
2 cloves garlic, peeled and crushed
½ cup water
1 bay leaf
½ teaspoon salt
1 teaspoon dry dill weed

Sterilize a pint canning jar and lid. Place the sliced cucumbers in the jar and set aside. Mix the remaining ingredients and bring to a boil. Once mixture comes to boil, strain, and pour over cucumbers and spices. Strain and pour over the cucumbers. Cover and refrigerate at least 2 hours. To serve, drain and serve cucumbers plain or on lettuce. Makes 1 pint.

Herbed Olives

MARSHA DEAN PHELTS

2 tablespoons capers, drained
2 teaspoons dried thyme
2 teaspoons crushed red pepper flakes
2 teaspoons dried oregano
4 bay leaves
½ teaspoon freshly ground black pepper
Grated zest of 1 lemon
Juice of 1 lemon
2–3 cups assorted olives, drained
Olive oil as needed to cover
2½ cup glass bottle or apothecary type jar with tight-fitting lid or top

In a small bowl combine capers, thyme, red pepper flakes, oregano, bay leaves, black pepper, lemon zest, and lemon juice. Place a layer of olives in the bottle and top with a tablespoon of the herb mixture. Alternate layers of olives and herb mixture, leaving ½ inch at the top. Fill with olive oil and seal with a sterilized lid or cork stopper. Allow the mixture to marinate in the refrigerator 10 to 12 days.

Marinated Mushrooms

MARSHA DEAN PHELTS

1 pound small button mushrooms
1½ teaspoons lemon juice or white vinegar mixed in 2 cups water
1 cup water
2 teaspoons salt
½ cup white vinegar
1 bay leaf
Thyme sprigs
1 garlic clove, peeled
2 tablespoons olive oil
Sliced green or mild red onion
Finely chopped parsley
Peel of 1 lemon, cut in thin strips

Trim mushroom stems and wipe the mushrooms with a cloth dipped in cold acidulated water (1½ teaspoons lemon juice or white vinegar to 2 cups water). Place the mushrooms in a heatproof bowl.

In a saucepan, combine 1 cup water, salt, vinegar, bay leaf, a few thyme sprigs, garlic, and oil. Bring to a boil. Remove from heat and pour over the mushrooms. Cool, then cover and refrigerate at least 12 hours, or up to 3 days.

To serve, drain mushrooms and discard bay leaf, thyme and garlic. Makes about 3 cups.

Pickled Eggs

MARSHA DEAN PHELTS

Juice from 1 16-ounce can beets
1 cup apple cider vinegar
½ cup firmly packed light brown sugar
6 whole cloves
1 stick cinnamon
6 hard-boiled eggs, peeled

Heat beet juice in a 1-quart saucepan. Add the remaining ingredients except eggs and simmer 10 minutes. Remove the cloves and cinnamon. Place the eggs in a sterilized 1-quart jar. Pour the hot liquid over and press a wad of plastic wrap onto the eggs to keep them submerged. Cool with the lid loosened. Close the lid tightly after eggs have cooled and refrigerate 4 days before serving.

Corn Relish

EVA R. LAMAR

8 ears fresh corn, white, yellow, or tricolor
2 red bell peppers, diced
2 green bell peppers, diced
2 medium onions, diced
½ cup sugar
4½ cups white vinegar
1 tablespoon mustard seeds
1 tablespoon salt
4 whole allspice

Sterilize 5 pint-size canning jars and lids and set aside.

Cut corn from the cob. Place all vegetables in a large pot. Add the remaining ingredients and cook over low heat until the sugar has dissolved, stirring constantly. Bring the mixture to a boil, stirring to prevent sticking or burning. Lower the heat and simmer 15 to 20 minutes, or until the vegetables are tender. Pour in hot sterilized jars. Seal tightly. The fruits of your labors are ready to be enjoyed.

Pickled Peaches

EVA R. LAMAR

4 pounds ripe peaches
2½ cups white wine vinegar
2 tablespoons whole peppercorns
1 teaspoon whole cloves
2 cinnamon sticks
5 cups sugar

Sterilize 4 pint-size canning jars and lids and set aside.

Blanch peaches in boiling water 30 to 40 seconds; timing depends on fruit's ripeness. Remove the peaches and immediately place in cold water. Drain and dry well. Peel and pit the peaches and set aside.

In a large pot bring the vinegar and spices to a boil. Reduce the heat and add the sugar; stir over low heat until the sugar dissolves. Bring the liquid to a boil and boil 2 minutes. Lower the heat and add the peaches; cook about 5 minutes. Remove the peaches and place in hot sterilized jars. Continue boiling the syrup a few minutes longer, until it is has reduced slightly. Pour it over the peaches, making sure they are completely covered. Seal the jars. Keep in a cool, dark place to strengthen the flavors. Makes 4 pints.

Preserved Kumquats

MARSHA DEAN PHELTS

5 pounds sugar
3 quarts water
5–6 quarts kumquats, washed and pricked

Sterilize ½-pint canning jars and lids and set aside. Combine the sugar and water in a saucepan and place over low heat. In another pot, bring the kumquats to a boil in enough water to cover, lower heat, and cook 10 minutes. Drain and put kumquats into hot syrup. Cook until liquid is clear and transparent. Let stand overnight.

Pack in sterilized jars. To process, place sealed jars in tepid water and bring to a boil. Let remain in boiling water 10 to 15 minutes.

23

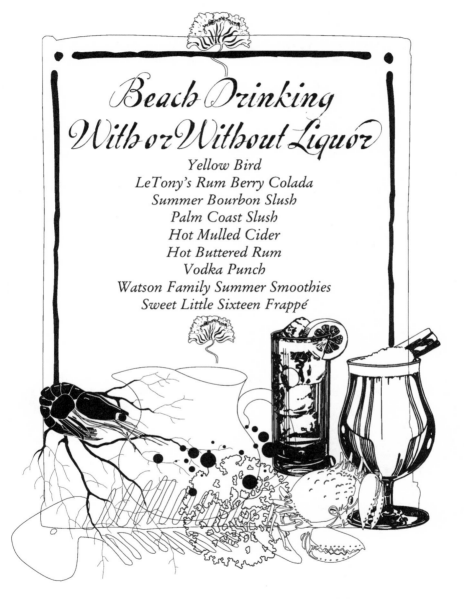

Beach Drinking
With or Without Liquor

Yellow Bird
LeTony's Rum Berry Colada
Summer Bourbon Slush
Palm Coast Slush
Hot Mulled Cider
Hot Buttered Rum
Vodka Punch
Watson Family Summer Smoothies
Sweet Little Sixteen Frappé

*If the ocean was whiskey / And I was a duck, / I'd dive to the bottom /
And drink my way up.*

FRANK PROFFITT

A merican Beach is a good, relaxing place to enjoy savory cocktails. These recipes call for a minimal amount of alcohol yet they are downright delectable. The recipes in this chapter burst with flavor. In many of these drinks you can leave out the alcohol and still have a luscious beverage. The few drinks included are seasonal favorites. Public safety announcements caution people against heavy drinking in extremely hot or cold weather.

⁓

My Big Mama was not a liquor drinker like me; however, she kept liquor in her house for medicinal and culinary use. One afternoon in the early 1970s, I stopped by to chat. We were sitting in the rocking chairs that spread across her front porch. Big Mama and I were speaking animatedly when, much to my surprise and delight, she asked if I wanted a cup of liquor. "Did I want a cup of liquor?" I thought. "This is my lucky day; Big Mama wants to get rid of some of the old brown liquor in the pantry."

My bottle tree.

"Why, yes, ma'am, indeed, I do want a cup of liquor." I happily followed Big Mama into the kitchen. She went to the cupboard, pulled down a thick coffee cup and rinsed it out. Then she removed the lid from a big pot on the stove and ladled the cup full of pot liquor—all that remained from the collard greens that had been eaten before I arrived. With extreme disappointment, I sipped that lackluster cup of green pot liquor, getting it down as quickly as I could. I should have known that Big Mama wasn't serving any liquor except that which provided sustenance.

~

Yellow bird is a drink that a host can serve and guests can enjoy without being overtaken by strong intoxicating liquors. A friend and neighbor, Merritt Hardy, shared this recipe with me. Merritt's recipe makes one eight-ounce serving. I've increased the amounts because once the number of liqueurs required have been purchased, it's easier to make a batch to serve or preserve. Follow Hardy's recipe and your guests will thank you for resurrecting precious memories of Paradise Island in the Grand Bahamas.

Yellow Bird

MERRITT HARDY

A fifth, liter, or quart of dark rum
½ pint crème de banana (Dekuyper brand, Natural Banana Flavor
    Crème De Banana)
½ pint Galliano
½ gallon fresh orange juice
½ gallon pineapple juice
½ pint fresh lemon juice
Pineapple tips, for garnish

Mix all ingredients and shake well. For each drink, pour over 8 ounces of crushed ice. Garnish with a pineapple tip. Makes 25 drinks.
Tip: This drink keeps well in the refrigerator or freezer. It is made in a big batch for convenience and is worth every cent spent for the flavors of the tropics.

LeTony's Rum Berry Colada

LETONY SESSIONS

1 pint fresh or frozen strawberries
1 15-ounce can cream of coconut
3 cups pineapple juice, chilled
3 cups club soda, chilled
1 pint coconut rum

Place strawberries and cream of coconut in a blender and puree on high speed until smooth. Pour in a large pitcher and mix with the remaining ingredients. Pour over crushed ice. Then sip, sip, sip. Please resist the temptation to guzzle. Serves 12.

Summer Bourbon Slush

EDNA M. CALHOUN

This is another mild-flavored beverage to sip on slow summer evenings while watching the lights of fireflies and listening to the croaking of frogs and the singing of cicadas. Summer bourbon slush is like an adult Icee—deliciously refreshing with a slow kick.
2 tea bags
1 cup boiling water
1 cup sugar
3½ cups water
1 6-ounce can (⅔ cup) frozen orange juice concentrate, thawed
1 cup bourbon
3 ounces (⅓ cup) frozen lemonade concentrate, thawed
Lemon slices

Steep tea bags in the boiling water 3 minutes; remove. Stir in the sugar. Add the remaining ingredients and stir until the sugar is dissolved. Pour into freezer containers and freeze firm. Remove from the freezer about 10 minutes before serving. Spoon the slush into cocktail glasses and garnish with lemon slices. Keep unused portion frozen. Makes 2 quarts.

Palm Coast Slush

EDNA M. CALHOUN

1 cup fresh orange juice
1 cup pineapple juice
1 cup whiskey sour mix
1 cup bourbon
½ cup crushed pineapple

Place all ingredients in plastic jug or pitcher with lid. Shake and put container in freezer overnight. Shake two or three times while freezing in order that pineapple bits will spread through the drink and will not settle on the bottom. Serves 4.

Hot Mulled Cider

MARSHA DEAN PHELTS

¼ cup firmly packed light brown sugar
1 quart apple cider or apple juice
½ cup spiced rum
½ teaspoon grated orange peel
¼ cup fresh orange juice
¼ teaspoon whole cloves
2 whole allspice
3 3-inch cinnamon sticks
1 tablespoon lemon juice
Dash ground nutmeg

In a medium saucepan over low heat, dissolve the brown sugar in the cider or apple juice. Add the remaining ingredients and simmer, uncovered, about 20 minutes; do not boil. Strain and discard the spices. Serve hot in punch cups with cinnamon stick stirrers, if desired. Makes 6–8 servings.

We seldom get to use this old recipe because weekends and holiday seasons are rarely cold enough for drinking heated liquor. But when it freezes in northeast Florida this makes a fabulous toddy to sip by the fireplace.

Hot Buttered Rum

MARSHA DEAN PHELTS

1 stick butter or margarine
½ cup firmly packed dark brown sugar
½ teaspoon ground nutmeg
½ teaspoon ground cinnamon
½ teaspoon ground cloves
Salt
Spiced or dark rum
1 lemon, thinly sliced

Combine the butter or margarine and brown sugar, whisking until light and fluffy. Add the spices and a dash of salt.

For each drink, put 2 teaspoons butter mixture and a jigger (¼ cup) of spiced or dark rum in a warmed 8-ounce mug and fill with hot water. Drop a twist of lemon in each mug. In this recipe, A twist of lemon is a thin slice of lemon, twisted to extract the juice in the mug to flavor the drink. Serves 8-12.

Vodka Punch

MARSHA DEAN PHELTS

1 cup sugar
2 cups water
4 cinnamon sticks
12 whole cloves
4 cups 100% cranberry juice
½–1 cups frozen lemonade concentrate, thawed
2 cups fresh orange juice
2 cups pineapple juice
1 quart ginger ale
1 quart vodka
Citrus fruit, for garnish

Bring the sugar, water, cinnamon sticks, cloves, and cranberry juice to a boil. Lower the heat and simmer 5 minutes. Refrigerate overnight. Next day, remove the spices and add the lemonade, orange juice, pineapple juice, ginger ale, and vodka.

Pour the mixture in a punch bowl and garnish with citrus fruit floats. Serves 16.

Watson Family Summer Smoothies

NINA WATSON

3 frozen bananas
5–7 big chunks fresh pineapple
¼ cup frozen blueberries
3 ounces unsweetened 100% cranberry juice
1 cup fresh orange juice

Blend all ingredients in a blender at high speed. Serves 2.

Sweet Little Sixteen Frappé

MARSHA DEAN PHELTS

2 10-ounce packages frozen sliced strawberries, or
1 quart chopped fresh strawberries
2 6-ounce cans frozen pink lemonade, thawed
2 cups water
1 quart strawberry ice cream
1 liter ginger ale

Put the strawberries in a blender and puree until smooth. Add the remaining ingredients except the ginger ale and blend briefly. When ready to serve, pour the blended ingredients into a cold punch bowl and add the ginger ale. Serves 16.

Home Remedies and Quick Fix Poultices of Bygone Years

Big Mama's Old–fashion Cold Remedy
Garlic Vinegar Teachers' Tonic
Anxiety Hot Lemon Tea
To Cure a Sore Throat
To Reduce Swelling
To Stop Bleeding
To Cure Mumps
Nature's Salve for Burns, Insect Bites, Poison Ivy
Nail Injuries
Turpentine Potion
To Break a Fever
Aunt Sue's Good for What Ails You
and Other Healing Remedies
Suggestions

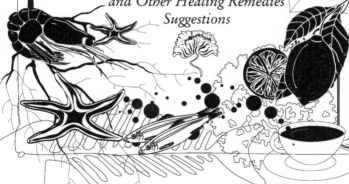

Folk medicine is practiced by a great number of persons.

ZORA NEALE HURSTON

The making of home brew, moonshine, and home remedies to cure ailments were a major operation in this area. Although we have entered the twenty-first century, many folk around here remember making their own libations. Bobby Jones remembers assisting his grandmother in the 1950s to make home brew at their home in Kraft Town, at the northern end of Amelia Island. Bobby's dad worked at the paper mill, and they lived in Kraft Town, within walking distance of the then Kraft Mill.

Bobby's first job in helping with the home brew was to get from the store one pack of barley, hops, and yeast. His grandmother added sugar, raisins, and peeled and diced white potatoes. She added half as much water as she had ingredients. This concoction was left to ferment for a month in a crock with a rag tied over the top. After a month of sitting in the corner of the back porch, the ripened beverage was strained and ready for revelry, with a small portion set aside for medicinal use.

Many times I have been under the weather, and when I can't find relief from the agony of a cold, virus, or rundown feeling, I get on the phone and call my mama or her baby sister Vera and their friends for their "never too late to mend" solutions. I have confidence in these remedies, for through the years they have all worked for me.

To treat your ailments, I advise that you go to the doctor. Enjoy this chapter for its historical value, for I am not representing myself as a physician or a pharmacist. I do, however, want to preserve our medicinal remedies and folk tradition for posterity. Once these folk medicines have been forgotten, they will be forever gone.

Big Mama's Old-fashioned Cold Remedy

AGNES LLOYD COBB

3 ounces fresh lemon juice
3 ounces honey
3 ounces hard liquor

Shake all ingredients in a jar until completely blended. Take 2 ounces twice a day and stay in bed until you are better.

❧

Deloris Gilyard shared this remedy with me for a pick-me-up. This concoction actually works; however, in order for me to remember to take this strong and bitter dose of vinegar and garlic, my body and mind have to be dragging me down. Since I retired in 2002, I haven't had a need for this remedy, but I know firsthand of its rejuvenating powers.

Garlic Vinegar Teachers' Tonic

DELORIS GILYARD

Place 12 freshly peeled garlic cloves in a 16-ounce container of vinegar. Drink an ounce of this concoction a day.

When you find that a sore throat is in full force and refuses to budge, try this concoction, which a colleague shared with me. You'll soon have control of your throat and vocal cords as yellow wads of phlegm dislodge.

Anxiety Hot Lemon Tea

CORA ROYAL HACKLEY

1 juicy lemon
2 cups water
1–2 cough drops or peppermint balls

Wash the lemon well and cut in half. Squeeze the juice in a saucepan with the water and the squeezed lemon halves . Bring to a boil and boil a minute or two. Drop the cough drops or peppermints in the mixture and steep 3 to 4 minutes. Pour in a mug and drink while warm.

Lemon tea without sugar or peppermint is also good for anxiety.

To Cure a Sore Throat

SHIRLEY MIKEL MEEKS

Gargle with warm saltwater.

To Reduce Swelling

SHIRLEY MIKEL MEEKS

Mix a cup of red clay into a paste using kerosene or turpentine. Apply the paste to the swollen area and tie a white cloth around it.

To Stop Bleeding

EVA R. LAMAR

As children, my brothers and I often had scrapes and minor cuts that bled. Mama's solution was to cover the wound with spiderwebs to stop the bleeding, and it worked. Spiderwebs worked just like a bandage. We weren't concerned about germs, only about stopping the bleeding.

My American Beach neighbor Carlton McKenzie, also known as "Spider Man" has been carrying that moniker since he was six years old. Carlton fell while running with a gallon jar of pickles. He was severely cut and scarred. There was no money to take him to the doctor, and health insurance was unheard of. Carlton's mother made a plaster of spiderwebs across his chest and it stopped the bleeding, though the scars from that day remain a half century later.

To Cure Mumps

To ease the pain of the mumps, anoint the swollen area between the ears, throat, and chin with oil from a can of sardines. Wrap with a clean white cloth. Reanoint as needed and wrap with a clean white cloth.

Living on the beach, mishaps with insects, poisonous stings, and minor burns frequently occur. Aloe plants are commonly relied upon for instant relief.

Nature's Salve for Burns, Insect Bites, Poison Ivy

Snap a portion of the leaf from an aloe plant and rub the gel that it exudes on the wounded area. This brings soothing relief quicker than anything you can buy across the counter.

Nail Injuries

When we punctured our feet with rusty nails while playing, Mama and Daddy didn't take us to Dr. E. H. Washington's office for treatment. The injured foot was washed. A penny was placed over the wound and covered by a slice of fatback bacon to draw the poisons out, then the foot was tied in a white rag (a piece of old sheet) or cheesecloth. Once the injury healed, the penny could be spent at the neighborhood/corner store by the wounded soul.

Turpentine Potion

We kept a bottle of turpentine in our medicine cabinet. A teaspoon of sugar with a few drops of turpentine was good for something—I can't remember what, and neither can Mama, but we often had to swallow a dose of this remedy.

To Break a Fever

To break a fever, a patch made from folded brown paper was soaked in vinegar and placed on the head.

Aunt Sue's Good for What Ails You and Other Healing Remedies

Throughout my childhood my daddy's sister, Aunt Sue, was a nurse in Amityville, New York. When my Aunt Marion became sick in 1953 and the doctors couldn't help her, Aunt Sue dispensed remedies with love and faith.

Susan Rosier Fawcett wrote in a letter, "For Marion: Take about six fresh mullein leaves. Cut them on the breadboard; then wash thoroughly. Put into a pot and simmer. That is, start on a low flame and let the pot of leaves and water come slowly to the boiling point. Use about a gallon of water (let simmer for one half hour or more). Then strain through something quite thick like a piece of sheet or Indian head so that none of the fuzzy comes through. Pour the hot brew over about three thick lemon slices, some orange peels and some raisins and about ½ to ¾ of a pint of sugar. Cover the container and let stand over night. The next day put into ½ gallon wine jug, some peach kernels or a few cherries, also one whiskey glass of whiskey. Then fill the bottle with the liquid, which stood over night. Screw top on bottle and place in the refrigerator.

Dose:

Take two whiskey glasses three times a day as you would orange juice. It makes a pleasant drink. Never allow yourself to run out of it. If you follow

Aunt Sue and Uncle Jim Fawcett (1925).

closely, you will get rid of the enlarged heart and find your health greatly improved in other ways. It's a wonderful reducing remedy.

Suggestions

1. Use Wheatena instead of hominy grits.
2. Use rice instead of potatoes.
3. Use whole wheat and rye instead of white bread.
4. Use nonfattening salad dressing.
5. Make a habit of eating fresh raw fruit and vegetables.
6. Go to bed as early as you can.
7. Take a midday rest.
8. Listen only to relaxing radio programs.
9. Exercise your body anyway you can, as often as you can.

Contributors

American Beach property owners **Charles** and **Ernie Albert** are descendants of Amelia Island families. Charles served three times as mayor of the City of Fernandina. Ernie is volunteer librarian at the Peck Center, and both graduated from Peck High School in the 1950s.

Community activist **Carol Alexander** is president of the A. L. Lewis Historical Society and executive director of the Ritz Theatre and LaVilla Museum.

Amelia Island native **Willie Mae Hardy Ashley** is an author and local historian. The beautifully restored Willie Mae Ashley Auditorium in Peck Center is named in her honor.

Mattie Betsch was the paternal grandmother of Mavynne, Johnnetta, and John Betsch. For a short time in the 1940s her granddaughters lived with her in Washington, D.C.

Mavynne Betsch's voice became the most recognized advocate for the preservation of historic American Beach. Mavynne, the "Beach Lady" and great-granddaughter of A. L. Lewis, studied opera and performed in Germany in the 1950s.

In the 1950s **Norris "Nick" Biggins** of Cleveland Heights, Ohio, was a day-tripper to American Beach from his home in Waldo, Florida.

Clarethea Edwards Brooks has shared family homes on American Beach since her parents built two cottages here in the 1940s.

Congresswoman **Corrine Brown** of the 3rd Congressional District of Florida has vacationed at and visited American Beach with family and friends throughout her life and is a community supporter.

The late **Elvira Gibson Brown**, who recorded oral history for the Works Progress Administration (WPA) was a founding principle in the establishment of the Durkeeville Historical Society in Jacksonville, noted for her culinary skills and local history.

Sylvia Jenkins Brown was a classmate, friend, neighbor, and colleague.

The late **I. H. Burney** and his wife, **Miriam Cunningham Burney**, originally of Atlanta, honeymooned on American Beach in 1936 and built their vacation cottage there in 1960. Burney Park and Burney Road are named in honor of I. H. Burney, who served as president of the Afro-American Life Insurance Company from 1967 to 1975.

Roslyn Burrough is a soprano who has starred on Broadway and has sung around the world. Mary Lewis Betsch—the Beach Lady's mother—was Roslyn's first piano teacher. Roslyn, aka Auntie Roz, frequents American Beach.

Charlotte Woods Burwell is an American Beach snowbird from New York, where she served as a member of the Ulster County School Board and manager of the infamous Peg Leg Bates Country Club.

For many years **Comilla Bush**'s American Beach properties have served as headquarters for the annual outings of St. Stephen's AME Church and family reunions.

Edna M. Calhoun a celebrated leader and role model as Dean of Women and Dean for Residence Life at Florida A&M University in Tallahassee and Howard University in Washington, D.C., is best remembered by family and friends for her hospitality.

Susan and **David Caples** are the owners of Elizabeth Pointe Lodge, an oceanfront bed and breakfast, "one of the 50 great values in America" (*Money Magazine*).

Kathie Jefferson Carswell, chaplain for the American Beach Property Owners' Association, is a direct descendant of Franklin Town families on the southernmost point of Amelia Island.

Frances Jollivette-Chambers of Miami and her family were annual vacationers on American Beach in the 1950s. See **Cyrus Jollivette** on page 272.

Big Mama, **Agnes Lloyd Cobb** (1889–1980), is my maternal grandmother. Agnes and her husband, Randall, relocated their young family to Jacksonville from their Lake City, Florida, homestead in the mid-1920s.

Bud Coe, an Amelia Island architect and historic preservationist, drew the plans for the home that would replace the most recognized landmark home on American Beach, the Blue Palace.

Johnnetta Betsch Cole, aka "Sister President," served as president of Spelman College in Atlanta and Bennett College in Greensboro, N.C. She is the great-granddaughter of A. L. Lewis, a principal in the establishment of American Beach.

Andrew B. Coleman III, of Coleman Mortuary and Admiral Limousine Service, provides transportation to American Beach for special occasions such as my retirement celebration and class reunions.

Ronnie Dawson is a retired marine who lives on American Beach, where he spends his time fishing and playing drums with area jazz bands.

Kurt Elijah Dean is my teenaged grandson and has been a tremendous help to me. Kurt has been coming to American Beach all of his life and enjoys fishing and crabbing with the family.

Kyle Dean has been coming to American Beach since before he could crawl or talk. I am his mother and greatly depend upon him to help with entertaining and providing hospitality for family and guests.

Mamie Shephard Delaney and her husband, James "Jack," are island-born, Mamie on the southern tip at the Harrison Plantation and James on the northern end in Old Town.

Eugene K. Emory, a psychologist at Emory University, went on a buying spree in the 1980s after taking a nostalgic drive through American Beach and finding many properties for sale. American Beach was his summer hangout during his college days at Edward Waters College in Jacksonville.

Susan Rosier Fawcett, a nurse in Amityville, N.Y., was my daddy's sister. Our family knew her for the advice and remedies she dispensed on healthy lifestyles. For me, Aunt Sue's cuisine was too healthy to be savory.

Neil Frink, president of the Association for the Study and Preservation of African American History of Nassau County and vice-president of the A. L. Lewis Historical Society, descends from a pioneering family in Amelia Island's fishing industry. Neil and his wife, Joyce, are active throughout the Florida First Coast.

Vera Cobb Gibson, my aunt, is fondly remembered for keeping folk practices alive for the family and neighbors.

Deloris Gilyard is an award-winning teacher and widely heralded as the island's caterer. Deloris and husband, Erving, have been permanent residents of American Beach for more than thirty years. Erving is a Nassau County native.

Torrie Gilyard, an American Beach native who earned a degree in hospitality from the University of Central Florida, is an asset to the Gilyard Enterprise.

Aunt Liza, aka **Eliza Rosier Glass**, a former caterer, is my paternal aunt. She passed on her cookbook collection to me in 1974.

Caruther (Ruth) Godwin, a retired nurse, spent many summers vacationing on American Beach with her family.

Harriett Bazzell Graham was a second-generation employee of the Afro-American Life Insurance Company and was long a part of the American Beach community.

Frances Green married into the Franklin Town family of **George Green**. The Greens trace their roots on the southern end of the island before the Civil War.

Alma Greene, a native Floridian from the panhandle, has become one of the newest homeowners in American Beach.

Metro Smith Griffith, who lives in a historic home, has been a part of the American Beach community since childhood.

Cora Royal Hackley of Jacksonville is a regular visitor and supporter of the many American Beach causes and projects.

Merritt Hardy is a third-generation resident of Amelia Island.

Lougenia Jackson Harris and her husband, James, are authorities on cooking, shell crafts, and island history.

The **Harris Teeter Grocery** store near the southern end of Amelia Island is the only store from the chain that remains in the state of Florida.

Lisa Harter is the owner of La Bodega Courtyard Café in the historic district of Fernandina Beach.

Willie Mae Hayes, a native of Jacksonville, and her husband, John, are longtime residents of American Beach.

Sarah Heath is a certified physician's assistant in Jacksonville who enjoys jaunts with her husband, Barry, to American Beach.

Nellie Ragland Henry, a soloist and pianist, and her husband, **Joseph Nathaniel Henry**, retired undersheriff from Jacksonville, enjoy their toy collection on the tree-lined streets of American Beach. They in-line skate, ride motor scooters, swim, and walk everywhere.

Alexander Hickson is a talented resident of both American Beach and Ohio.

LaShonda Jewel Holloway, a Jacksonville native who resides in Washington, D.C., is building a vacation home on American Beach.

The **Rev. William "Bill" Holmes** and his wife, Altamease, are Amelia Island natives who render valuable religious, educational, cultural, and civic services.

The late **Daisy Brookins Hunter**'s family was among the first residents of American Beach. The homes that her father, S. A. Brookins, designed and built on American Beach still stand.

Lois and **Jerry Iszard** are longtime residents. The Iszards are known and appreciated for hospitality. Jerry is a pharmacist by profession and photographer by interest.

The late **Evelyn Green Jefferson** is a native of Franklin Town. The home that she and her husband, William, built in 1965 was moved to American Beach in 1972 from Franklin Town.

Cyrus Jollivette, a vice-president of Blue Cross Blue Shield of Florida, frequently vacationed on American Beach during his childhood with his parents, Frances Jollivette-Chambers and the late Dr. Jollivette.

Barbara and **Carlton Jones** are community activists and philanthropists. Carlton, publisher of the *People's Advocate* weekly newspaper and developer of the Gateway Shopping Center, is serving his second term as president of the American Beach Property Owners' Association, Inc.

Evelyn Jones, a retired certified physician's assistant, works with diligence to beautify the community entrances and roadway.

Francina Carter King's family has owned vacation properties on American Beach since 1942.

The late **Charles Kirtsey** was an Amelia Island pioneer who retired from the Rayonier Paper Mill.

Claire Koshar of Central Florida trains and shows labrador retrievers.

Ron Kurtz is a noted Amelia Island author and historian.

Eva R. Lamar is my mother and has nurtured the family's passion and appreciation of American Beach. She is a nonagenarian, an avid bridge player, and a lifetime member of the Mt. Sinai Baptist Church.

Gwendolyn Leapheart has been a part of the American Beach enclave from its development in 1935 and remains a vital community servant.

As office manager for the Atlanta Life Insurance Company, the late **Netty Leapheart** frequently brought clients to American Beach.

Norma Leuthold, a retired secretary from the Duval County School System is the mother of my architect and former students William Jr. and Scott.

The late **Elsie Manning Lohman** lived a few miles north of American Beach at the bluff on the Amelia River. In 1935 her husband, Rudolph Jr.(deceased), helped his father install the plumbing in the first homes and facilities built on American Beach.

Janie Cowart Madry was the last teacher in the one-room schoolhouse in Franklin Town. Janie and her family were home- and property owners in the community.

Beverly and **Carlton McKenzie** recently constructed a three-story ocean-view American Beach home. Their three children also assisted in this family project.

As a teenager, during the American Beach Golden Age of the 1950s and 1960s, **Virginia McKinney Mealing** worked in many of her family's lodging and restaurant businesses on American Beach. She and her husband, Jessie, relocated to the island in 2000.

Shirley Mikel Meeks is a frequent beachgoer on American Beach.

Since moving to American Beach in 2003 **Ronald Miller**, who retired from CSX, spends his time as a baseball umpire across the state. Ron, a surf fisherman, and his wife, Lynnette Young, are noted for the quality and frequency of their hospitality.

Jeanette Mobley, a third-generation islander, grew the vegetables that she served in her American Beach restaurant, Net's Place.

Emma Holley Morgan, who first came to American beach in 1945, is an institution in this community. The Morgans (Frank Sr. and Emma) were the last operators of the ocean-view parking lot fondly remembered as the jumping-off place for tailgate parties.

Debra and **Gregory Morrison**, of Deluth, Ga., are among the newest American Beach residents and maintain the Web site www.historicamericanbeach.com.

Annette McCollough Myers, author of *The Shrinking Sands of an African American Beach*, is a native-born Amelia Islander. Myers served as president of the American Beach Property Owners' Association. Myers launched and completed the project that resulted in the listing of American Beach in the National Register of Historic Places on January 28, 2002.

Janis Owens, a novelist, and her husband, **Wendel**, live in rural North Florida.

Larney Owens and his wife, Lill, live in Atlanta with their two sons. Ancestors of the Owens family bought into the development of American Beach early on in the founding years.

Upstate New Yorkers **Dorothy Patrick** and her late husband, **Robert**, became homeowners on American Beach the first time they laid eyes on the community in the 1990s.

Belva Burney Pettiford is the daughter of I. H. and Miriam Cunningham Burney. Belva and her sister, Miriam Stamps, along with their families, continue to enjoy American Beach.

Margaret Bennett Peyton is a Jacksonville native with family ties to American Beach.

Michael Phelts, my husband, makes many contributions to the community with his photography.

Joyce Robinson and her husband, **James**, have gone on more than fifty cruises since moving full time to American Beach in the 1980s. The Robinsons filed and won a racial discrimination lawsuit in 1998 against Domino's Pizza. A federal judge ordered Domino's to provide home delivery to American Beach as long as pizza continued to be delivered to Amelia Island Plantation.

Gloria Davis Roderick and her five siblings worked in all capacities at the Duck Inn, which her late parents, Granderson and Cora Davis, owned and operated on American Beach. This historic structure, where Mary McLeod Bethune resided during visits to American Beach, remains a family property. Gloria and her husband, Charlie, now reside in American Beach.

Marvin Rooks was principal of the Arlington Elementary School in Jacksonville throughout the 1970s and frequently prepared fudge to the delight of the staff.

Charles Rosier Sr. (1913–1987), my father, was an avid fisherman who brought the family and our dogs to American Beach the first two weeks in July for our summer vacation.

Kenneth Rosier, my younger brother, recently fulfilled a longtime goal when he made a pilgrimage to Mecca. A Muslim, he is known as Kenneth Diaab Mahdi.

Dori Sanders is an acclaimed author who lives on the family farm in York, South Carolina, where she operates a peach orchard.

The late **Charlie Savage**, grandfather of my former student Juan Savage, shared much sought after spices that he brought home from his travels as a merchant seaman.

Saveur Magazine is a gourmet food magazine with recipes and cooking techniques that make cooking a cultural adventure.

Pearlie Scarborough is my aunt and was noted among family and friends for her baked goods.

Bonnie Matthews Scott along with her husband, **Willie C. Scott**, have a beach home in the Stewartville Community and have been on the American Beach scene for over a half century.

LeTony Sessions, an Amelia Island native, is the owner/operator of Hair Works by LeTony.

Marie Sessions served on the board of trustees for American Beach, Inc. in the 1990s.

Dolores Ponder Shaw and her family serve as hosts for their family reunions on American Beach and the First Coast.

Sayre Sheldon came to know and love American Beach through her brother, the late Bradley Phillips, a landscape and portrait painter.

Terri Singletary and **Cheryl L. Wright** are the owners of Classic Creations Full Service Catering.

Dennis Stewart, aka Mr. Natural, is a noted and creative chef. Dennis and his brother Michael are grand children of Ralph and Marie Taylor Stewart, who recruited many original property owners to invest in American Beach.

Michael Stewart, the organizer of the Virgo Bash Celebrations held in the 1980s and the 1990s, was awarded the Boy Scouts for Life Saving and the Bell South Vale Award for saving a man from drowning on American Beach in 1991.

From her blue pickup truck **Mary Stewart**, aka "Mrs. Mary Fannie" of Stewartville, picks up and drops off surplus produce to the delight of family and neighbors all over the island.

Velma Stewart, daughter of "Mrs. Mary Fannie," married Duke Stewart (unrelated), thus remaining a Stewart. Velma and Duke live on Stewart Street in Stewartville.

William "Bill" Strain has been coming to American Beach since it began and has been living here since his retirement from the City of Jacksonville in 1969.

The late **Melba Brookins Sunday** and her husband, Philip, began their careers as instructors at Edward Waters College after their wedding in

1937. Melba's father, S. A. Brookins, designed and built homes for each of his three children when they married.

He Shorty (deceased) and his wife, She Shorty (**Samuel** and **Almetha Thompson**), were my American Beach running partners. I also learned invaluable pointers about entertaining from this couple.

Shelia Walker is noted for her culinary and cake baking skills as she assists her brother and sister-in-law, Erving and Deloris Gilyard, in their catering enterprise.

Viola Walker, romance writer, relocated from Detroit, Michigan, to American Beach after retiring as grants writer for the Detroit School System.

Nina Watson, a pharmacist, helped her father, William Watson, build his three-story American Beach home.

Lisa Vander Wege is the owner of the only restaurant in operation on American Beach. This popular eatery, Gourmet Gourmet, lives up to its name and was voted one of the best restaurants on Florida's First Coast in 2006 and 2007.

Index

248; peaches, 250; shrimp, 55; watermelon rind, 247

Pies and cobblers, 226–34; berry duby, 233; grape, 230; key lime, 226; lemon, 227; mango pineapple casserole, 234; orange blossom, 228; orange meringue, Florida, 228; peach cobbler, 231; Mrs. Mary's cheesy tomato, 98; Mrs. Mary's sweet tomato, 232

Pigs' feet, He Shorty's, 45

Poison ivy treatment, 264

Pompano en papillotte, 157

Potatoes, 101–6; hash brown casserole, 106; Margaret's pride, 106; sinful potatoes, 105; stewed, 104; stuffed new potatoes, 104. *See also* Potato salad

Potatoes, sweet, 107–13; boats, 111; candied, 112; cream cheese pie, 110; pone, 108; pudding, 112, 113; soufflé, 109

Potato salad: German, 103; southern shrimp, 103

Poultry, 163–73; chicken and scampi, 167; chicken curry, maharani, 170; chicken tetrazzini, 172; chicken livers, chopped, 44; chicken livers, deep-fried, 44; con pollo, Daddy Charlie's Jamaican, 173; curried chicken, Aunt Liza's, 169; late-night chicken pot, 165; pressed chicken, 172; southern fried chicken, Momma's, 165; stewed chicken and cornbread dumplings, 168

Preserving, 245–51

Pressed chicken, 172

Puddings: banana, creamy, 205; bread, Nama's, 203; sweet potato, 112, 113

Punch bowl cake, 213

Quiche, American Beach, 19

Ratatouille, 89

Red and white blue fish, 159

Red deviled spiced shrimp, 53

Red snapper chowder, 31

Red Snapper with Smashin' Salsa, 155

Red velvet cake, 210

Rice: fresh vegetable, 99; Mrs. Morgan's dressing, 99; orange, 126

Robinson, Joyce, 218–19

Roderick, Gloria Davis, 38

Rooks, Marvin, 196

Rosier, Charles, Sr., 24, 80–81

Rosier, Kenneth, 187

Salads, 63–74; ambrosia, 65; Christmas pea, 70; confetti, 70; cornbread, 66; cottage cheese, Aunt Liza's, 73; cranberry, 65; crustacean cocktail, 69; deviled tomatoes, 73; Emma's pole bean, 74; fruit, 68; fruit of the sea, 151; garden, 72; German potato, 103; Green Derby special house, 71; grilled fruit, 68; island fruit, 67; southern shrimp potato, 103; spinach, 72

Salmon cakes, 21

Sandbar crab cakes, 122

Sanders, Dori, 231

Sandwich platter, 83

Sandwiches, 75–83; cucumber, 82; eggplant, 79; fishwich, 77; fried tomato cream cheese, 83; leftover liver, 81; leftover shrimp, 80; peanut butter and honey raisin, 82; sandwich platter, 83; veggiewich, 78

Savage, Charlie, 173

Savory crab-shrimp gumbo exotica, 29

Scampi Ron, 135

Scarborough, Pearlie, 231

Seafood: conch, cracked (fried), 126; oysters, crisp fried, 127; paella, Fran's, 148; seafood and vegetable batter, 142; seafood casserole, Aunt Liza's, 119; seafood creole, 145
–crab: crab, with garlic parsley, 125; chafing-dish crab, 125; crab boil, soul man's, 149; crab cakes, 122; crab-shrimp bake, 146
–shrimp: coconut-fried, 133; crustacean delicacy, 132; Easter surprise, 135; with feta, 134; fruit of the sea (shrimp, scallops, squid), 151; smothered, 131; sweet-sour, 146; shrimp and sausage fettuccine, 139; shrimp creole, 145; shrimp Delores with sauce, 140; shrimp purlo, 138; shrimp salsa and brown rice, 137; shrimp chops, crab-coated, 133; shrimp scampi, 135

Sessions, LeTony, 189, 256

Sessions, Marie, 181–82

Shaw, Dolores P., 90

She-crab soup, 27

Sheldon, Sayre, 25–26

Shrimp and sausage fettuccine, 139

Shrimp creole, 145

Shrimp Delores with sauce, 140

Shrimp dip, 51

Shrimp purlo, 138

Shrimp salsa and brown rice, 137

Marsha Dean Phelts, a retired school and public librarian, is a full-time resident of American Beach, where she is active in the community. She is the author of *An American Beach for African Americans*. Marsha and her husband, Michael, are freelance writers and photographers for *The Florida Star* newspaper.